The HarperCollins Concise Dictionary of English Usage

THE HARPERCOLLINS CONCISE DICTIONARY OF

ENGLISH USAGE

Eugene Ehrlich and Daniel Murphy

Series Editor, Eugene Ehrlich

HarperPerennial

A Division of HarperCollins*Publishers*

ISBN 0-06-271526-7
ISBN 0-06-461025-X (pbk.)
Library of Congress 90-55994

91 92 93 94 95 MAC/MB 5 4 3 2 1

*This book is dedicated to Mrs. Eileen Murphy,
whose husband, Daniel J. Murphy, was my colleague
and friend for more than 30 years. Dan's death came
shortly after completion of this, our final collaboration.*
                                    Eugene Ehrlich

PREFACE

In compiling this dictionary of usage, we have had several goals in mind. Above all, we wanted to give understandable and authoritative answers to questions that writers and students of writing ask most often. With this in mind, we have supplied illustrative examples to augment our discussions. Secondly, we wanted to make each discussion easy to locate and as complete as possible in a concise dictionary, so readers do not have to search elsewhere for definitions of the grammatical and stylistic terms we use. Finally, we wanted to make our discussions as lively as possible for readers seeking help. *The HarperCollins Concise Dictionary of English Usage*, therefore, presents in alphabetical order certain principles, precepts, practices, and prejudices—our own—in matters of syntax and style. And it does so in language as direct and as lively as we can manage. We leave to our readers the final word on whether we have served them faithfully.

E. E.
D. M.

The HarperCollins Concise Dictionary of English Usage

A

ABBREVIATION

While abbreviations are permissible in informal writing—personal letters, class notes, stories using familiar language—they should be used sparingly in papers or documents requiring formal English. In footnotes and bibliographies, abbreviations are used extensively. Abbreviations are most appropriate in publications in which space is at a premium: business reports, manuals, and reference books. The best example of a publication in which space is at a premium is a telephone directory.

Commonly Used Abbreviations

Mr., Mrs., Dr., M.D., B.A., and Ph.D. are commonly used with names: Mrs. James Jackson, B.A.; Alfred Nieman, M.D. We never write, "He is a Dr.," since an abbreviation is not used to designate a group or class. Names of familiar agencies (S.E.C. and C.I.A.) are usually abbreviated, and the periods within the abbreviations may be omitted (SEC and CIA). A.D., B.C., etc., a.m., and p.m. are almost never given except as abbreviations. When used with a name, Professor and other titles are abbreviated if the first name or initials of the person are supplied: Professor Hughes, Prof. E.F. Hughes; Reverend Wilkins, Rev. T.S. Wilkins. The abbreviation Ms. is used now to designate a woman without reference to her marital status. This designation has the appearance of an abbreviation, but no one knows what it stands for.

Scholarly Abbreviations

English has many abbreviations for words used frequently in scholarly writing, particularly in bibliographic entries.

[1] Cleanth Brooks and Robert Penn Warren, *Modern Rhetoric,* 2nd. ed. (New York, 1949), p. 47.

[2] Thomas Mann, *The Holy Sinner,* trans. H.T. Lowe-Porter (New York, 1951), p. 9.

[3] *Ibid.,* p. 94.

The trend in scholarly writing is to avoid using abbreviations. In any formal writing, therefore, with the exception of certain scholarly journals, these abbreviations should not be used, since many readers do not know the meanings intended. If you are going to use abbreviations in your documentation of formal papers or articles, you should be familiar with the most common abbreviations:

Abbreviation	Latin Meaning	Meaning
c., ca.	*circa*	about or around (referring to dates or time)
cf.	*confer*	compare
cm.		centimeter
ed.		editor, edition, edited by
e.g.	*exempli gratia*	for example
et al.	*et alii, et alios*	and others
et seq.	*et sequens*	and the following
ff		(and) the following pages
fig.		figure
fl.	*floruit*	flourished
ibid.	*ibidem*	in the aforementioned place
i.e.	*id est*	that is
il., illus.		illustration, illustrated by
loc. cit.	*loco citato*	in the place cited
MS, MSS		manuscript, manuscripts
n.d.		no date given
n.s.		new series
No.		number
op. cit.	*opere citato*	in the work cited
p., pp.		page, pages
q.v.	*quod vide*	which see
repr.		reprinted
rev.		revised, revised by
s.		series
sup.		supplement, supplements
tr.		translation, translated by
vol., vols.		volume, volumes

Two other terms used by scholars deserve mention here even though they are not abbreviations: *passim*—in different sections of a text cited without specific reference to pages; and *sic*—thus—which signifies that material has been quoted correctly even though it appears to contain an error. In this use *sic* is always enclosed in brackets.

Dictionaries may supply abbreviations in a special list, as entries in the main listing following the word abbreviated, or as separate entries. When in doubt about an abbreviation, consult a current dictionary.

Periods with Abbreviations

Except in special cases, listed below, abbreviations are followed by periods.

- Periods are frequently omitted in the abbreviations for government agencies, labor unions, airlines, and the like—FBI, TWA, CBS, AFL-CIO.
- Acronyms, abbreviations pronounced as words, are not punctuated—UNESCO, NATO, OPEC, radar, loran.

The best advice about whether to abbreviate a term is: *When in doubt, spell it out.*

ADJECTIVE

An adjective is a word used to modify, limit, or describe another word or group of words performing a noun function. Adjectives modify subjects, objects, objects of prepositions, gerunds, and noun clauses:

- The *stone* wall was built to conform with the *oval* configuration of the driveway. (*Stone* modifies *wall. Oval* modifies *configuration.*)
- The *glaring* lights blinded the driver of the *speeding* car. (*Glaring* modifies *lights. Speeding* modifies *car.*)
- A *red, green,* and *blue* sash identifies the leaders of the group. (*Red, green*, and *blue* modify *sash.*)

Someone once said that adjectives are the death of nouns. What this means is that a great deal of uneven and careless writing results from excessive use of adjectives. A precise noun does not need adjectives.

Comparison of Adjectives

Adjectives can be cast in forms that reflect degrees of the characteristic being communicated. This is done by adding *er* or *est* to the positive form of some adjectives and by placing the words *more* or *most* before the positive form of other adjectives.

Positive	Comparative	Superlative
friendly	friendlier	friendliest
friendly	more friendly	most friendly
fat	fatter	fattest
small	smaller	smallest

Position of Adjectives

An adjective may be placed before or after the noun it modifies. In simple modification the adjective usually precedes the noun.

- *small* pony, *rigid* structure, *open* door

Adjectives may follow the word modified (1) in order to achieve emphasis, (2) because of a pattern inherited from another language, or (3) because the adjective is itself modified, and placing it before the word modified would be awkward.

Emphasis
A tour *complete* for two hundred dollars.
The country, *divided*, was on the verge of civil war.

Pattern from Another Language
attorney *general*, court-*martial*, secretary-*general*

Adjective Itself Modified
a design so *intricate* (The adverb *so* modifies *intricate*. The adjective *intricate* modifies *design*.)
a plan infinitely *complex* (The adverb *infinitely* modifies *complex*. The adjective *complex* modifies *plan*.)

ADVERB

An adverb modifies verbs, adjectives, and other adverbs.

- She hit the ball *sharply*. (*Sharply* modifies the verb *hit*.)
- They were *unrealistically* optimistic. (The adverb *unrealistically* modifies the adjective *optimistic*.)
- The charges were drawn *extremely* narrowly. (The adverb *extremely* modifies the adverb *narrowly*.)

You sometimes can eliminate adverbs by selecting a precise verb. For example, the sentence "She hit the ball sharply" can be written without an adverb.

- She *smashed* the ball.

- She *whacked* the ball.
- She *pounded* the ball.

Form of Adverbs

Most adverbs end in *ly,* but a handful—derived mainly from Old English—do not have any special adverbial sign: *now, quite, then, there, when, yes,* and *no.*

Comparison of Adverbs

(See ADJECTIVE for discussion of degrees of comparison.) Some adverbs show degrees of comparison by adding *er* or *est,* others by placing *more* or *most* before the adverb. Words that are used as adjectives as well as adverbs form their comparatives and superlatives in the same way.

Positive	Comparative	Superlative
deep	deeper	deepest
deeply	deeper	deepest

Deep can be both adverb and adjective.

- Mary fell *deep* in debt. (adverb)
- A *deep* decline in the stock market affects the entire economy. (adjective)
- The couple fell *deeper* in debt. (adverb)
- A *deeper* decline in the stock is expected. (adjective)
- They fell *deepest* in debt when their children were born. (adverb)
- The *deepest* decline came recently. (adjective)

Deeply is always an adverb.

- They apparently were *deeply* hurt. (The adverb *deeply* modifies the adjective *hurt.*)
- They were *more deeply* hurt than I expected.
- She was hurt *most deeply.*

It is worthwhile to consider three other examples of comparison of adverbs.

Positive	Comparative	Superlative
timidly	more timidly	most timidly
happily	more happily	most happily
badly	worse	worst

- She performed *badly* on opening night.
- Her accompanist performed *worse.*

- The chorus performed *worst* of all.

The three examples just given show the adverb *badly* in its three forms. Read on.

Adverb-Adjective Confusion: Badly & Bad

Confusion of *badly* and *bad* is a common error in writing and speech. *Badly* is an adverb; *bad* is an adjective.

- My daughter-in-law drives *badly*. (The adverb *badly* modifies the verb *drives*.)
- Her husband is a *bad* driver. (The adjective *bad* modifies the noun *driver*.)

Writers ordinarily have no trouble with *badly* and *bad* in sentences such as these. Trouble arises when a LINKING VERB, also called copulative verb, is used.

Incorrect I *felt badly* only after I left my bed that morning. (A linking verb, such as *feel* or *be*, cannot be modified by *badly* or any other adverb. A linking verb takes a complement, either an adjective or a noun. In this case an adjective would be appropriate.)

Correct I *felt bad* only after I left my bed that morning. (The adjective complement *bad* is correct.)

Adverb-Adjective Confusion: Well & Good

What has been said about the proper uses of *badly* and *bad* applies as well to *well* and *good*.

| well | better | best |
| good | better | best |

While *good* functions as an adjective, *well* functions both as an adverb and an adjective.

- Considering the poverty in which the children were reared, they did *well* to complete grade school. (In this sentence, *well* modifies the verb *did*, so *well* here is an adverb.)
- After they practiced, they performed *better* than most people expected. (The adverb *better* modifies the verb *performed*.)
- We ate *best* when the regular cook was absent. (The adverb *best* modifies the verb *ate*.)
- They felt *well* by evening. (The adjective *well* complements the linking verb *felt*.)

- She was *better* late in the day. (The adjective *better* complements the linking verb *was*.)
- She seemed *best* in the morning. (The adjective *best* complements the linking verb *seemed*.)

Identifying Adverbs in a Sentence

A simple formula identifies adverbs and adverbial phrases and clauses in a sentence

- With the same bat, the shortstop yesterday smashed the ball out of the park.
  The verb is *smashed*:
- Smashed where? *out of the park*
- Smashed how? *with the same bat*
- Smashed when? *yesterday*

If we desired, we might also have answered the question Smashed why?—*to get a raise*.

Position of Adverbs

Adverbs and adverbial constructions have no fixed position in an English sentence. Single-word adverbs should be placed as closely as possible to the word or group of words they modify.

- She *certainly* failed.
- The boat crashed *heavily* on the rocks.
- He *almost* finished the examination.

Adverbial phrases and clauses precede or follow the main statement; however, the order in which these modifiers are placed can vary, as shown in five versions of the same sentence:

- *Before the woman could reach the door,* the rain splashed *furiously around her.*
- *Before the woman could reach the door,* the rain splashed *around her furiously.*
- The rain splashed *furiously around the woman before she could reach the door.*
- The rain splashed *around the woman furiously before she could reach the door.*
- *Around the woman* the rain splashed *furiously before she could reach the door.*

When you are trying different sentence patterns in your writing, remember that adverbial constructions can be moved rather freely to enable you to achieve the rhythm and flow desired. Think carefully about the effects you are trying to achieve when you choose patterns for your sentences.

AFFECT, EFFECT

The simplest means of distinguishing between these troublesome words is to remember that *effect* is normally a noun meaning a *result*, and that *affect* is normally a verb meaning *influence*.

- The *effect* of the experiment encouraged the scientists. (noun functioning as subject of verb *encouraged*)
- The accident did not *affect* the result of the race. (verb)

In formal English, *effect* is sometimes used as a verb meaning *bring about*, usually in the passive voice.

- The result *was effected* by several means.

This use of *effect* as a verb is overdone in scientific and technical writing, thus contributing to the weakness and dullness of much of this writing. Writers would do well to rediscover the verb *cause* and try using it whenever they are inclined to use *effect* as a verb.

In psychology *affect* is sometimes used as a noun meaning *emotion* or *feeling*.

- Blunted *affect* may sometimes be a precursor of serious mental illness.

AGREEMENT

Of all the syntactical problems that plague the writer, agreement is one of the most annoying. (Can problems of agreement be so widespread because logic is becoming rare in our lives?) Yet questions of agreement can always be resolved by using logical analysis to reveal what is intended in a sentence.

Subject and Verb

Subject and verb must agree in number. When a subject is singular, its verb must also be singular. When a subject is plural, its verb must also be plural.

- The *woman wants* to do the best job she can. (singular)
- Most *men and women have returned* home long before nightfall. (plural)

- Even *animals show* more kindness than many supervisors. (plural)
- *Registration* in a drug program *guarantees* nothing. (singular)
- The *criterion is* simple enough to apply. (singular)
- The *criteria are* too vague to apply. (plural)
- *Formulas* (or *formulae*) *exist* for solving most of those problems. (plural)

Be careful to maintain agreement when dealing with a plural noun or noun phrase that follows a LINKING VERB, such as any form of the verb *be*. Remember: the verb must agree with its *subject*, not with its *complement*.

- *Prudence is* the heart and soul of his nature.
- The patient's *heart* and *liver are* the focus of the study.

In these two examples, the subjects are *Prudence*, a singular, and *heart* and *liver*, a plural. The noun phrase *heart and soul* in the first sentence may appear to be plural—the question of whether it is will be discussed shortly—but it is not subject of the verb. *Heart and soul* is the noun complement of the verb *is*. In the second sentence, the noun *focus* is singular, but it is not the subject of the verb. *Focus* is the noun complement of the verb *are*. Now observe what happens when the sentences are rewritten.

- The *heart and soul* of his nature *is* prudence.
- The *focus* of the study *is* the patient's heart and liver.

In the first rewritten sentence, it becomes apparent immediately that *heart and soul* offers the reader two nouns, *heart* and *soul*, linked together to convey but a single thought. You might well have written *essence* and thrown *heart and soul* into the receptacle where you keep your supply of discarded clichés. Anyone who would write "The heart and soul of his nature *are* prudence" would be in deep trouble. Of course, *heart* and *soul* may be used as a plural with separate meanings: "The discussion of the distinction between *heart* and *soul* droned on."

In the second rewritten sentence, *heart and liver* must be treated as plural. (Ask anyone who needs a liver or heart transplant—a heart is one thing, a liver another.) Even so, the question of whether the verb should be *are* rather than *is* has nothing to do with *heart and liver*. The verb agrees with its subject, *focus*, not with the complement, *the patient's heart and liver*.

If you use a construction that appears awkward, identify the subject of the verb and then make certain the verb agrees in number with the subject. If that does not make things clear, avoid the construction. Anything that looks awkward to a writer will mystify a reader.

Anyone on the way to becoming a good writer will always try to avoid using a pair of words where one word will do just as well. In the example using *heart and soul*, nothing is added to the thought conveyed by coupling *soul* with *heart*. The two words do have separate meanings, but not as they are used in this sentence. Other examples of this idle coupling include *happy and overjoyed*, *thrilled and elated*, *sad and dejected*—why bother to go on? The point to be learned here is that a verb must agree with its subject rather than with its complement, and this is better illustrated by using a real coupling of subjects:

- *Honesty* and *forthrightness* of expression *were* the hallmark of the frontiersman. (These are two distinct qualities.)
- *Ham* and *eggs has* always *been* a favorite at the American breakfast table. (Yet it is correct to say, "*Eggs* and *ham are* staples of the American diet." Here we are not thinking of ham and eggs as a single dish, but of eggs and ham as two different foods.)

Up to this point in the discussion, we have dealt with agreement in simple sentences. Complex sentences introduce another element of difficulty.

You have just seen how the number of the subject in an independent clause determines the number of the verb in that clause. Now remember that the number of the subject of a relative clause determines the number of the verb in that clause.

- May is one of our teachers *who have contributed* to learned journals.

The inference drawn from this sentence is that May is not the only one of our teachers who have contributed to learned journals. The subject of the relative clause is *who*, and the antecedent of *who* is *teachers*. Since *teachers* is plural, *who* must be plural. Therefore, the verb must be a plural, *have contributed*. This becomes clear when we rewrite the sentence:

- Of our teachers who have contributed to learned journals, May is one. (Of course, we would never write the sentence in this way except to test agreement.)

Now consider this sentence:

- May is the only one of our teachers *who has contributed* to learned journals. (Here the antecedent of *who* is *one*. We could not rewrite this sentence as: Of our teachers who has—or *have*, for that matter—contributed to learned journals, May is the only one. It is clear that no one else has contributed to learned journals.)

- May is our only teacher *who has contributed* to learned journals.

When the parts of a subject are joined by *or* or *nor*, the verb must agree with the subject closest to it.

- Either he or I *am* to blame. (The problem of agreement here goes beyond that of deciding whether the verb is to be singular or plural. Since *I* is first person singular, the verb must be *am*, which is also first person singular. It would be incorrect to write, "Either I or he *am* to blame." It would be grammatically correct to write, "Either I or he *is* to blame," but the practice of putting other people before ourselves is so ingrained that writing *I or he* would be considered incorrect.)
- Neither the mathematician nor the physicist *is* ready to disclose the findings of the experiment.
- Neither she nor her sisters *are* going to the party.

Pronouns, Possessive Adjectives and Their Referents

A pronoun must agree with its antecedent in gender, number, and person—a concept demonstrated partially in the above sentences dealing with the teacher who writes for learned journals.

- The boys are anxious about the fair *they* have planned. (The pronoun *they* agrees in number with its referent, *boys*.)
- The generals, *who* were not consulted, now find *themselves* shouldering all the blame. (The pronoun *who* has *generals* as its referent, so *who* is plural; the pronoun *themselves* also has *generals* as its referent, so *themselves* is also plural.)
- Danny will find out that, despite all the support the other boys are giving, *his* opinion will not be honored. (The possessive adjective *his* is singular because its referent, *Danny*, is singular.)
- *What* you will find is that most of your class will be fast asleep by the time you have completed your lecture. (*What* is singular because its referent is singular: *that most of your class will be fast asleep by the time you have completed your lecture.*)

Problems arise when pronoun and antecedent are widely separated in a sentence or when one or more words might logically be referred to. By analyzing a sentence grammatically, these faults can be corrected.

- The problems he habitually left for solution early in the morning—when a cup of coffee seemed to fortify his first rush of energy with the desire to work—were *those* involving calculus. (*Those*, not *that*. But, of course, you will avoid writing sentences as rambling as this one. For example, you might write, "He habitually left for early morning problems such as those involving calculus. It was then that a cup of coffee seemed to fortify his first rush of energy with the desire to work.")

Another problem involves the use of pronouns that have as their antecedents such pronouns as *each*, *another*, *anyone*, *somebody*, and *everybody*. These five pronouns are all singular and therefore take singular verbs. Any pronoun using one of the five as antecedent must also be singular.

- *Everybody* wants *his* own way in the matter.
- *Anyone* who is of age can vote for *her* favorite candidate.

The pronoun *none*, which is also singular, is under constant pressure. Consider the following situation:

- Ten member nations are expected to send delegates to a meeting of the World Health Organization. Because of an international crisis, however, all stay away.

In reporting this incident, do you write:

- *None* of them *attend* the meeting.
- *None* of them *attends* the meeting.

While *none* is as singular as anything can be—after all, it means *not one*, and *one* is singular—all but the strictest of grammarians would say *none attend*. By now *none* as a singular has practically lost the battle. We are reduced to a situation in which we can insist on a puristic stand and risk sounding stuffy in many cases, or we can go along with the times, or we can avoid the construction. And avoiding a troublesome situation is better than insisting on raising questions in the minds of our readers.

ALLITERATION

Alliteration is the term used to denote the deliberate repetition of similar consonant sounds. The repetition of sounds for artistic effect is practiced mainly in poetry, but it can be used effectively in prose as well.

When to the *sessions* of *sweet silent* thought
I *summon* up remembrance of things past,
I *sigh* the lack of many a thing I *sought*
—Shakespeare, Sonnet XXX

The *fair* *breeze* *b*lew, the white *f*oam *f*lew,
The *f*urrow *f*ollowed *f*ree
—Coleridge, *Rime of the Ancient Mariner*

*K*indly and *c*lear-sighted ... un*c*ontaminated by their *s*qualor
and *c*onfusion, *c*ourageous and firm in his *c*lear allegiances amid
the flu*x* of things, a pale angel at the *C*arnival....
—Santayana, "Dickens"

While you may be tempted at times to try your hand at alliteration
in a prose passage you are writing, be aware that the situation must
be right for a device so striking. And such situations seldom seem—.
Never mind.

ALL RIGHT

This is the correct spelling. *Alright, allright,* and *all-right* are all
wrong.

AMBIGUITY

A sentence that can be understood in more than one way is an
ambiguous sentence. And ambiguity is an undesirable condition that
should be repaired through careful rewriting. Ask yourself, What am
I talking about? Make the subject you are writing about the subject of
your sentence. Then ask, What am I saying—predicating—about it?
Make that the main verb—the predicate. In this way the logical and
grammatical subjects coincide, and the logical and grammatical verbs
coincide.

If there is a Murphy's First Law of Writing, it is this: *Anything that
can be misunderstood will be misunderstood.*

Amount, Number

Amount is used for things thought of in bulk, *number* for things
counted:

- the *amount* of electricity, gas, ink, paper, sugar, tea, or wood
  used
- the *number* of lamps, pens, plywood panels, term papers in our
  possession

AMPERSAND

The ampersand (&) is primarily a space-saving device, used appropriately in informal business writing and lengthy reference works. It

is not used properly in formal writing. If you are quoting from a text, you must use the ampersand if the text uses it.

AND

And has three grammatical functions: (1) to link independent clauses; (2) to connect parallel constructions (adjectives, adverbs, nouns, verbs, verbals, phrases, and clauses); and (3) to indicate the final element in a series.

Independent Clauses

When *and* is used to join two independent clauses, *and* is always preceded by a comma.

* Tamara decided to go fishing, and Norma said she would go along to watch. (You can always determine whether a clause is independent. Try putting a period before the *and*. When the result is a complete sentence, the clause is independent.)

Parallel Structure

And connects any two similar grammatical units.

* black and white print
* pen and pencil
* the man who likes to write and to talk
* whatever pleased his senses and whatever shocked his friends

Series

And, preceded by a comma, is used before the final element in a series. Although many newspapers, magazines, and much informal writing have stopped using the comma before *and*, formal writing retains it.

Formal There is no feeling for adventure, romantic love, and sentimentality.

Informal There is no feeling for adventure, romantic love and sentimentality.

Incorrect Use of AND

Poor writing often uses *and* as a connective where no connective is needed or where a different connective would be more suitable.

Poor None of the elective courses seemed attractive, *and* no one registered for them. (Although these two clauses are independent grammatically, the thoughts expressed are closely related as to cause and effect. *And* does not convey this relationship. One of the clauses should be made subordinate to the other and then connected by a suitable connective.)

Improved Since none of the elective courses seemed attractive, no one registered for them. (The opening clause is subordinate.)

Improved None of the elective courses seemed attractive, *so* no one registered for them. (Now the second clause is subordinate.)

Improved Because none of the elective courses seemed attractive, no one registered for them.

Poor The sales manager offered no bonuses to salesmen, *and* his competitors did. (The sentence seems to want to contrast the thoughts of the clauses. The conjunction *and* does not achieve this intent.)

Improved The sales manager offered no bonuses to salesmen, *but* his competitors did.

Improved Although the sales manager did not offer bonuses to his salesmen, his competitors did.

Improved Even though the sales manager's competitors offered bonuses, he did not.

The word *and* is often considered incorrect when it is the first word of a sentence. A sentence can open with any word, but in formal writing *and* or other coordinating conjunctions are used to open sentences only to achieve a deliberate stylistic effect. (The sharp-eyed reader has already seen examples of such use in this book.)

- No solution seemed possible, and Harry knew it.
- No solution seemed possible. And Harry knew it.

(Both sentences are correct, and it is left to you to decide which you prefer.)

ANTECEDENT

An antecedent, also known as a referent, is the word or group of words to which a pronoun refers.

- Because the *Braddocks* were exhausted, *they* went to sleep. (*Braddocks* is the antecedent of *they*.)
- The *referees* decided that *they* would go along with the desires of the majority. (*Referees* is the antecedent of *they*.)

15

Beginning writers are apt to fall into the *Trap of the Ambiguous Pronoun*. This reckless endangerment to understanding awaits those who use apparently innocent words—*he*, *she*, *it*, and *they*—without providing a clue to the antecedents that support these pronouns. Without easy access to the correct antecedents, readers do not know which way to turn.

Such ambiguity—not to mention the bewilderment and frustration it may induce—can be avoided. First of all, careful writers keep pronouns close to their antecedents. Secondly, they eliminate all unnecessary pronouns. Finally, they never place a word or phrase that can be misconstrued as an antecedent between a pronoun and its true antecedent. Consider the following examples:

- Juliet told Helene *she* was not permitted to attend the performance. (Who was not permitted to attend the performance? Only *she* knows, and she is not telling.)

  Improved Helene was told she was not permitted to attend the performance. (Only one possible antecedent: *Helene*. Pronoun: *she*, almost directly following its antecedent. The person who informed Helene has been removed from the sentence.)

  Improved According to *Juliet*, Helene was not permitted to attend the performance. (Pronouns eliminated. Now we also know who told Helene. Discussion closed.)

- Henry informed Jim that *he* will not be allowed to write a thesis until *his* grades improve. (Who will not be allowed to write a thesis, *Jim* or *Henry*? Not only is the pronoun *he* in trouble, but the POSSESSIVE ADJECTIVE *his* is equallly ambiguous. Does it refer to *Henry* or to *Jim*? There is no way of telling.)

  Improved According to Henry, Jim will not be allowed to write a thesis unless *his* grades improve. (Antecedent: *Jim*, the only word preceding the possessive adjective *his* that can serve as its antecedent. Pronoun *he* has been eliminated.)

Don't think for a moment that excellent writers instinctively avoid the *Trap of the Ambiguous Pronoun*. During the process of writing a first draft, even excellent writers make errors. When these writers complete a draft, however, they go through it carefully, and one of the things they try to do during that reading is make certain that their sentences are free of ambiguity. (Notice that the previous sentence uses the pronoun *they* twice and the possessive adjective *their* once. There is no doubt that *they* and *their* refer to *writers*. There are no

other people in the sentence, so there are no other possible
antecedents.)

ANTONYM

An antonym is a word that has a meaning approximately the opposite of another word.

- hot and cold
- black and white
- soft and hard

APOSTROPHE

The apostrophe (') is the mark of punctuation used to indicate the
possessive case in nouns, the omission of letters in contractions, and
dropped letters in reported speech. An apostrophe is also used in
forming the plural of a letter or a number.

Genitives or Possessives

The singular of a possessive is formed by adding *'s* to the base word,
the plural by adding the apostrophe after the final *s*—if there is one.

- a boy's book, a girl's hat, an hour's delay
- three hours' delay, men's clothing, women's careers

In the best writing, the apostrophe is used to show possession only
for people and time.

Incorrect the table's legs
Correct the table legs, the legs of the table

When a name ending in *s* requires an apostrophe to show possession, add an *s* after the apostrophe unless the resulting word offends
the ear.

- *Yeats's* plays, but not *Euripides's* plays (*Euripides'* plays is far
  more pleasant.)

Contractions

The apostrophe indicates omission of one or more letters in contractions.

- isn't, wouldn't, can't, I'll

The most common error is the confusion of *it's* (meaning *it is*) with
its, which is the possessive form of *it* and means *belonging to it.*

- It's more than a body can bear.

- It's as much my fault as his.
- Its success is far from certain.
- Soon enough, the roof collapsed, its timbers eaten through by carpenter ants.

Reported Speech

The apostrophe is used to indicate that certain sounds that ordinarily appear in a word were not spoken:

- "John is *goin'* and he *ain't comin'* back," she said. (The words *goin'* and *comin'* lack the final *g*. The apostrophe in *ain't* has a more complex explanation. The evidence is that there once was the form *amn't*, which was a contraction of *am not*. Centuries of use of *amn't* in speech gave us the form *ain't*, with the apostrophe considered a replacement for the letter *o*. What the future of this word will bring is unknown, but you can be certain that teachers and editors for a long time will consider *ain't* unfit for formal writing—except in the case of reported speech.)

Plurals

An apostrophe and the letter *s* are used to form the plural of a letter or a number, although modern editors often drop the apostrophe when forming the plural of a number.

- Two *e's*, not two *i's* are needed in that word.
- Who among us did not rejoice when the *1980's* (or *1980s*) came to a conclusion?

APPOSITION

Apposition is a construction in which a word or group of words complements or supplements another. When an appositive is *restrictive*—when it limits the element it complements—it is not punctuated. When an appositive is *nonrestrictive*—when it does not limit the element it complements—it is punctuated.

- William the Conqueror (There are many Williams, so *the Conqueror* limits *William*—it is restrictive—and is not punctuated.)
- William the Conqueror, King of England and France, is admired even today. (William is already limited by *the Conqueror,* so the second appositive, *King of England and France*, is nonrestrictive and is set off by commas.)

- A lexicographer I particularly admired died recently. (*I particularly admired* limits the noun *lexicographer*, making *I particularly admired* a restrictive appositive and so not set off by commas.)
- My uncle Ben, who lived in Brooklyn, was a tailor. (The punctuation of this sentence tells us that there is only one uncle Ben in this family, *my* uncle Ben, so *who lived in Brooklyn* is a nonrestrictive appositive.)

ASSONANCE

Assonance is the term used to denote the deliberate repetition of similar vowel sounds. Like ALLITERATION, assonance is used primarily in poetry, but it is also an effective device in prose.

> Therefore a secret unrest
> Tortured thee, brilliant and bold!
> Therefore triumph itself
> Tasted amiss to thy soul.
> Therefore with blood of thy foes,
> Trickled in secret thine own.
> —Arnold, *Heine's Grave*

> I cannot forecast to you the action of Russia. It is a riddle wrapped in a mystery inside an enigma.
> —Winston Churchill

ASTERISK

An asterisk (*) is used sometimes to call a reader's attention to the presence of a footnote in a paper that has few footnotes. Asterisks can also indicate an omission from a quotation or the absence of lines from a quoted poem. In some works asterisks are used to indicate cross references.

ATTRIBUTIVE

An adjective standing next to a noun is classified as attributive.

- the *small* boy, the *yellow* submarine, a *golden* opportunity, a *splendid* opportunity
- the man *passionate* but *disinterested*, an opportunity *lost*

Nouns used as adjectives are also attributive.

- the *stone* wall, the *glass* door, a *term* paper

AUXILIARY VERB

An auxiliary verb is used with another verb to form tense, mood, or voice.

- The ship *has been* standing in the harbor for days.
- She *will* be happy when she completes all her examinations.
- You really *should* follow her lead.
- Young parents find soon enough that their advice seldom *is* obeyed by their children.

(See TENSE, MOOD, and VOICE.)

AWKWARD

Awkward is a term applied by cranky critics—more often by composition teachers—to writing that is stylistically inadequate. The term indicates that, although no specific rule of grammar has been violated, the writer's message is obscure or ambiguous. The label *awkward* most often means that the writing is loaded with DEADWOOD or marked by illogical word order, sloppy DICTION, or slack and flabby sentence structure. The remedy is rewriting. Search out all deadwood, correct any faulty diction, and tighten sentence structure. Keep in mind that *direct* writing is seldom awkward: Ask yourself how you would express a given thought if you were asked a direct question by someone standing in front of you. The answer will be direct, and your writing can become just as direct.

B

BAD, BADLY

The confusion between *bad* and *badly* in everyday speech is rivaled only by the confusion between *good* and *well*. Who has not heard "I feel *badly* about..." as a response to a question beginning, "What do you think of...." The problem is that *feel* in the sense intended by *feel badly* is a COPULATIVE, or linking, verb. That is, like *be* and *seem*, *feel* does not take an object—it usually does have a COMPLEMENT—nor can it be modified. Just as one cannot *be badly* or *seem badly*, one cannot *feel badly*.

(Like most grand statements, the one just made is not entirely true. If someone falls victim to a neurological disorder or similar handicapping condition, that person may lose the sense of touch. When loss of the sense of touch occurs, the afflicted person might legitimately—and correctly—say, "I feel badly.")

In any case the grammatical—or syntactical—function performed by a copulative verb is that of connecting subject and complement. Remember also that a copulative verb cannot be modified.

> *Incorrect* I told the doctor that I felt *badly* all day. (*Badly* is an adverb that appears to modify *felt*. The verb *felt* in the sense intended is a linking verb and cannot be modified.)
>
> *Correct* I have felt *bad* all day. (*Bad* is an adjective that functions here as a predicate complement.)
>
> *Correct* Unable to see anything in the dark, the prisoner *felt* her way along the dungeon wall. (The verb *felt* here takes an object, *wall*. Since *felt* is not acting as a copulative verb, it can be modified.)

BE

Be is the most frequently used of all English verbs and the most varied in its forms—*am*, *is*, *are*, *was*, *were*, *been*, etc. Writers have no trouble with the verb *be* except for choosing the case of the pronoun that follows *be* when *be* is used as a linking, or copulative, verb.

Should we say, "It is I" or "It is me"? When asked, "Who's there?" should we say, "I" or "Me"? The distinction is between the formal and the informal. In the formal we follow *be* with a pronoun in the subjective case. In the informal we follow *be* with a pronoun in the objective case.

BECAUSE

Informal it's me, it was him, that's her
Formal it is I, it was he, that is she

Forms of *be* are used with other verbs to form progressive tenses and to form the passive voice.

- I am walking, I have been walking, they will have been walking
- I was awakened, I had been awakened, they will be awakened, I will have been awakened

BECAUSE

Because is a subordinating conjunction that gives the reason for the action of the main statement.

- *Because* the entire team was tired and dispirited, no one was willing to go out last night.
- The house had to be torn down and rebuilt, *because* fire had gutted the structure.

Because does not follow such constructions as *the reason is* and *the explanation is*. Instead we say the reason is *that,* the explanation is *that.*

BI-, SEMI-

Wouldn't life be simpler for you as a writer if everybody accepted the idea that the combining form *bi-* means "two" and that the combining form *semi-* means "half"? (*Semi-* also has other meanings, as you will shortly see.) If people accepted the definitions given in the first sentence of this paragraph, nobody would question whether *biennial* and *biannual* mean "every two years" or whether they mean "twice a year." After all, a self-respecting dictionary would have to admit that *bi-* means "twice" as well as "two."

Over the centuries use of *biennial* and *biannual* and many other words employing *bi-* has thoroughly confused the situation. Writers, therefore, are well advised to avoid *biennial* and *biannual*. Instead they should use such phrases as "occurring twice a year" and "occurring every other year" and use equivalent phrases for other *bi-* words.

Things are less confused in the case of the large family of *semi-* words. No one apparently thinks that *semi-* means anything but "half," so there is no confusion over the intentions of *semiannual* and *semicircle*. The only additional consideration is that *semi-* has acquired the meanings of "incompletely," "partially," and "somewhat."

Languages are forever on a roll: Just when we think we have all nailed down the meaning of a word, people begin to attach additional meanings to it. Thus, in the case of *semi-* we now have "semidetached houses," "semiliquid states," and "semihardy plants." It would be folly to think of these phrases as being correctly interpreted as "half detached" or "half liquid" or "half hardy."

BRACKETS

Brackets ([ ]) are used in formal writing to indicate that some explanation or comment has been added to quoted material.

- "Much, however, has been done in the L[ane] matter that should not have been done, and much should be done if only B[lackwell] would lend a hand."

The quotation given here is faithful to the original text. The only change made is to complete two names that were abbreviated in the original text. Thus, what was given as *L* has been amplified to *Lane*, but the person who supplied the quotation has indicated the amplification for readers by supplying brackets: *L[ane]*. The same is true for *B[lackwell]*. Such amplifications are especially useful for modern readers, who may not be familiar with the details of historical events.

- "Should we be per[torn] to go ahead...."

Within the brackets appears the word *torn*, meaning that the page supplying the quoted material was torn, making part of the material unreadable. The writer might have speculated on what was missing and filled in the torn section. If the writer had done so, the material supplied would have been enclosed in brackets.

Here is a sentence in which the writer has seen fit to speculate on missing material:

- "Should we be per[mitted] to go ahead...."

Brackets are used with *sic* to indicate that an apparent error in a source is being reproduced exactly.

- "Several sources refuted the Pensylvania [sic] study." (The writer quoting this sentence does not want readers to think he misspelled Pennsylvania.)
- "The General Assembly found no dischrepancy [sic] in the revised test." (Comparable comment.)

Brackets are also used in footnotes to enclose material given inside parentheses.

BUT

- ... and that he had no desire to remain (*The Letters of W.B. Yeats*, ed. Allen Wade [New York, 1955], p. 72).

It is clear, then, that brackets are an *editor's* mark rather than a *writer's* mark. When writers use brackets, they are acting as editors of material they are incorporating into their own writing.

BUT

But is used as a coordinating conjunction, as a connective between two grammatically equal units, and as a preposition.

When *but* connects two independent clauses in opposition, it is preceded by a comma.

- Everyone agreed that the party had been a success, *but* no one wanted to clean up afterwards.
- Most people in the Middle East want lasting peace, *but* their leaders may have other goals.

When *but* connects grammatical units performing similar functions, be certain the units are grammatically equal—two words, two phrases, or two clauses:

- a virile *but* gentle man
- generous *but* affordable housing
- representing herself as submissive *but* actually harboring deep and understandable resentments
- ostensibly dancing to the music *but* actually following an inner rhythm
- He called for a national day of prayer *but* anticipated and got little response.
- She hoped that Emma would soon go home from the hospital *but* that she would obey her doctors' instructions to rest this time.

When used as a preposition, *but* is not preceded by a comma.

- Everyone wanted to go *but* Jim.
- We dug for three hours and found nothing *but* a few badly chipped arrowheads.

C

CAN, MAY

In formal writing it is advisable to continue to distinguish between the auxiliary verbs *can* and *may* even though popular usage has largely blurred the differences that formerly were commonly observed in the use of these two verbs. Thus, in formal writing we use the auxiliary verb *can* in the sense of "be able to" and the auxiliary verb *may* to express possibility, opportunity, permission, and the like.

- Even though difficulties still face women seeking employment as police officers, qualified women *can* usually manage to find jobs. (Women usually are able to find employment as police officers.)
- We know that it *may* rain tomorrow, but we intend to go forward with our plans. (There is always a possibility of rain, so one might say, "It *can* rain tomorrow." What is intended here, however, is to suggest the possibility of rain rather than the ability to rain.)

CAPITAL LETTERS

Almost everyone knows that the beginning of a sentence requires a capital letter and that proper names are capitalized, but some confusion exists among students and writers over other correct uses of capitalization in formal English. The following discussion covers the most common uses for capitalization.

Proper Names

Capitalize proper names of persons (Saddam Hussein, George Bush), places (Kuwait, Saskatchewan); races and nationalities (Oriental, Irish); rivers (Hudson, Ohio); days of the week (Friday, Sunday); months (July, September); names of companies (Dow Chemical Company, General Motors); fraternal organizations (Kiwanis); religious bodies (Church of God, Church of England); languages (Swahili, French); historical events (American Revolution, Battle of Hastings); and documents (Declaration of Independence, Magna Carta).

Do not capitalize the seasons or the points of the compass. In formal English capitalize the name of a region, despite the fact that most newspapers and some journals tend to use lower case letters.

- I promise to devote my entire *summer* to completing the project. (season)
- Go *east* for about two hundred miles, then *southeast by south* for fifty miles. (points of the compass)
- I spent most of my six months in the United States touring the *Far West*. (region)

Lines of Verse

Capitalize the initial letter of a line of verse unless the poet has chosen not to capitalize it.

> The sea is calm tonight,
> The tide is full, the moon lies fair
> Upon the Straits;—on the French coast, the light
> Gleams, and is gone; the cliffs of England stand,
> Glimmering and vast, out in the tranquil bay.
> Come to the window, sweet is the night air!
> —Arnold, "Dover Beach"

> love is a place
> & through this place of
> love move
> (with brightness of peace)
> all places
> yes is a world
> & in this world of
> yes live
> (skillfully curled)
> all worlds
> —e. e. cummings, "Poem 271"

Titles of Books, Plays, Articles, Essays, Poetry

Capitalize all words in a title except articles, conjunctions, and prepositions of less than five letters—unless these parts of speech occur in the first or last position in the title.

- *We Bombed in New Haven*
- *Reflections in a Golden Eye*

- "The Love Song of J. Alfred Prufrock"
- "The Lake Isle of Innisfree"
- *To Have and Have Not*
- *Two Against the Gods*

In titles that contain hyphenated words, capitalize if both parts of the hyphenated expression are nouns. A note of caution: If the author of a book has capitalized in a manner that does not agree with this rule, follow the author's practice. You are not obliged to correct authors.

- *Confessions of an English Opium-Eater*
- *Moby-Dick*
- *History of the English-speaking Peoples*

Titles of Persons Occupying High Office

Capitalize the name of the office whether or not the holder of the office is named.

- The President of the United States
- the Senator
- the Secretary of State
- the Prime Minister
- the Secretary-General

CARELESSNESS

Like spelling errors, all errors caused by carelessness are inexcusable. Careless errors are the mark of lazy, immature writing—the kind of writing that bedevils teachers, editors, and critics. Ignorance of a fine point of grammar or style may be understandable; carelessness is not. Most of the careless errors that creep into papers should be caught before the final revision, and for that reason writers should complete a project several days before the work is due, surely leaving plenty of time for a final retyping or unhurried final correction on a word processor.

Reviewing a paper several days after it has been written—just before final retyping or final correction on a word processor—gives writers a chance to read their work as though they had not seen it before, almost as a stranger will read it. They are thus more likely to catch errors. When an initial draft is completed only a few hours before a paper is due, fatigue combines with haste to guarantee careless errors in the completed paper.

CARET

The caret (∧) is the mark placed under or in a line of manuscript to indicate that something should be inserted at that point. The material to be inserted is written in the margin of a text that is to be submitted to a printer. In the case of student papers, the material to be inserted is more often inserted between the double-spaced lines of the paper:

- She is one of the most ∧ women I have ever known.

distinguished

CASE

Case expresses the relationship between a noun or pronoun and another element in a sentence. The cases of nouns give little difficulty—there are only the common form and the possessive.

- Common form: *boy, boys*
- Possessive form: *boy's, boys'*

A difficulty in establishing correct case occurs when determining the case of a pronoun following a linking verb. Informal English uses the *objective* (accusative) case, but formal English uses the *subjective* (nominative) case.

Here are examples of pronouns appearing after the linking verb *be*:

Formal It is I.
It is she.
It is he.
It is we.
It is they.

Informal It is me.
It is her.
It is him.
It is us.
It is them.

Another difficulty is the confusion between *who*, which is the subjective case, and *whom*, which is the objective case:

Informal the person *who* you were speaking to
Formal the person to *whom* you were speaking

Things get stickier in other constructions, as you will shortly see. It is worthwhile to open the discussion with a sentence that gives no one trouble and then go on to more difficult problems.

Correct She is the one *who* can give you directions. (*She* is in the subjective case because it is the subject of the verb *is* in the independent clause. In the subordinate clause, *who can give you directions*, the verb is *can give* and the subject of the verb is *who*, which is in the subjective case. If you wish, you may turn the subordinate clause into a question to see whether you have things right. Surely you would say, "Who can give you directions?" Surely you would not say, "Whom can give you directions?" Easy enough so far.)

Correct Percy is the one *whom* most people prefer. (This sentence has an independent clause, *Percy is the one*, and a subordinate clause, *whom most people prefer*. The verb in the dependent clause is *prefer*. Its subject is *people*. The verb *prefer* has an object, the pronoun *whom*. Pronouns acting as objects must be in the objective case. For this reason, *whom* is correct: *Most people prefer him*.)

Correct The actor *who* should have won the Oscar received only applause. (Independent clause: *The actor received only applause*. Subordinate clause: *who should have won the Oscar*. Verb of subordinate clause: *should have won*. Subject of verb: *who*. Since *who* is subjective, the sentence is correct.)

Incorrect The company official *whom* I thought would be fired received a bonus and a raise. (Subordinate clause: *whom I thought would be fired*. Verb: *would be fired*. Subject of verb: *whom*, which is in the objective case. The subject of verb must be in the subjective case. Would you say, I thought *him* would be fired?)

Correct The company official *who* I thought would be fired received a bonus and a raise. (Now we have a subject, *who*, of a verb, *would be fired*, that is correctly in the subjective case .)

Now consider the problem of the case of an object of a preposition. The rule is that the object of preposition must always be in the objective case.

Correct The college will offer scholarships *to them*.

Correct The contract is acceptable *to him and me*.

Incorrect I shall give this *to whomever* applies for it. (The pronoun *whoever* should be substituted here. The pronoun is not the object of *to*, but the subject of *applies*. The entire clause *whoever applies for it* is the object of *to*.)

In elliptical constructions—constructions from which something has been intentionally omitted—using *than* or *as*, the case of a pronoun is established by the use of the pronoun.

   Correct We can operate the snow plow as well as *they*. (The full sentence could have been *We can operate the snow plow as well as they can operate the snow plow*. Few people would write the sentence this way. The elliptical construction *We can operate the snow plow as well as they* is customary. Nevertheless, *they*, in the subjective case because it is the subject of the intentionally omitted verb *operate*, is correct. The objective *them* would be incorrect. You certainly would say, "They can operate the snow plow." You would certainly not say, "Them can operate the snow plow.")

   Correct The dean stayed later than *I*. (The verb intentionally omitted after *I* is *stayed*.)

   Correct I like you better than *her*. (I like you better than *I like* her.)

CHILDISH STYLE

Childish style is writing that presents disjointed claims in sentences that appear to have no logical connection. The assertions made are usually unsupported by hard fact. People who write in this manner seem to be haranguing readers instead of presenting carefully constructed argument. Such writers, perhaps because they are aware that their exposition is not convincing, characteristically fill their prose with multiple exclamation points, underscoring, the dots of ellipsis, unwarranted superlatives, and carelessly chosen adjectives. The intent may be to convey excitement and emphasis, but the result is failure. Empty stylistic devices and extravagant, unsupported claims do not convince readers. Readers are convinced by thorough explanation and logical development of ideas that are supported by facts.

CLARITY

Clarity is an essential quality of good prose style. In the process of trying to make yourself correctly and easily understood, you must pay special attention to sentence structure, diction, and logical presentation of ideas. Granted that certain ideas are inherently more difficult to understand than others, writers still must strive to achieve clarity no matter what subject they are discussing. College theme writers who claim that the profundity of their ideas excuses their lack of clarity are not apt to reach sympathetic ears. Since clarity is not ordinarily achieved in one pass, it is essential to examine and improve what you write before submitting it. Achievement of clarity is your responsibility, not your reader's.

To guarantee clarity in a piece you are about to write, begin by asking yourself what you are trying to tell your reader. Can you express your main thought in a sentence? Almost any idea can be expressed in a single English sentence, sometimes simple in construction, sometimes complex. As you think through what you want to say, write your thoughts down. Once you have established just what you want to say, you have your main idea. You then must ask yourself what additional thoughts and information are needed to develop and support your main idea. As these further thoughts occur to you, write them down in a list of words and phrases. When you believe you have everything you need, number the items in their logical order of presentation. *First I will discuss this, then I will discuss that*, and so on. Undoubtedly, here and there you will find gaps in your thinking. Whenever you recognize that you have a gap, fill it in. When your list is complete, you have a workable outline.

At that point, it is time to begin writing to your outline, expressing yourself in sentences composed of words that instantly come to mind to convey each thought. Do not spend time worrying over the quality of your expression. If you concern yourself at this stage with how well you are writing, you risk getting bogged down. Instead, concentrate on completing your first draft, on getting all your thoughts down on paper or in the memory of your word processor. Immortal prose will come later. If, while you are making your first draft, thoughts come to mind that you have overlooked in your initial planning, do not hesitate to depart from your outline. Get your new thoughts down. If you find that some elements of your original outline turn out to be phantom thoughts—items so insubstantial that they do not merit even a sentence in your first draft—skip right over them. There is nothing sacred about an outline.

It is a rare writer who can think through a piece of writing flawlessly before beginning to write. Experienced writers know that the act of writing immerses them in their subject and almost certainly enables them to come up with ideas they have overlooked in planning. They also know that the act of writing enables them to recognize that they have included elements in an outline that do not merit inclusion in the piece they are writing.

Of course, we have all had advice about outlining before now and we all know that planning and writing in this way will always be easier to say than do. We also know, however, that thousands of professional writers—journalists, essayists, magazine writers, reviewers, book writers—do their work daily and effectively. They also work under pressure, as student writers often do. So how do the professionals achieve an acceptable degree of clarity? The answer is that in writing their first drafts they may not even come close to building in the clarity they will eventually achieve. A first draft is not intended to yield polished prose, but it does get the writing process under way and provides the raw material needed for the final steps that result in clear writing.

So how do writers finally achieve clarity? Professional writers sometimes say that they are not writers, but rewriters. They have learned the disciple of going back over pieces they have written as many times as necessary to attain at last the effect they originally set out to achieve. Beginning with a first draft, professional writers become editors of their own work. If you follow their procedures, you will read with care each word in every sentence you have written, asking yourself whether you have always selected the right word to express what you mean, or whether a better word is needed. (Your dictionary will be invaluable here. Don't hesitate to consult it. If a better word does not come immediately to mind, you may have to consult a thesaurus, but you will use your dictionary to check any word you are thinking of using to make certain it means just what you think it means.) Will a reader understand each sentence easily? Have previous sentences prepared readers for the new thought expressed? Have the necessary connective elements been supplied? Does each sentence say what it should say? Indeed, does it say anything? Is it an unnecessary repetition of something said before? Does a word belong elsewhere in the paragraph in which it appears? Does a particular paragraph logically belong elsewhere?

Word processors make life easy for a writer—sentences, paragraphs, even entire sections can be moved almost effortlessly. There is no need for elaborate schemes of marking material to be moved. Scissors and tape can be discarded.

When you are satisfied that your readers will not have to puzzle over what you have written—that every word, sentence, and paragraph is chosen carefully and placed precisely where it belongs so that your presentation is logical—you surely will have achieved clarity.

The message is clear: Rewrite, rewrite—each time examining what you have written from the point of view of a reader who is reading your work for the first time.

CLAUSE

A clause is a group of words having a subject and predicate. An *independent clause* may stand alone as a sentence.

- She drank two cups of tea to be polite, but her husband refused to drink any. (Two independent clauses connected by *but*, a coordinating conjunction. Try making a sentence of each clause: *She drank two cups of tea to be polite. Her husband refused to drink any.* Both clauses have a subject and predicate. The clauses are independent.)

A *subordinate clause*, also called a *dependent clause*, may not stand alone as a sentence. It must be joined to some other element in a sentence by a relative pronoun or a subordinating conjunction, whether present in the sentence or understood.

- Several of the alumni who visited the campus were astonished by its new beauty. (The independent clause *Several of the alumni were astonished by its new beauty* can stand alone as a sentence. The subordinate clause *who visited the campus* cannot—unless it is changed to a question: *Who visited the campus?* The relative pronoun *who* serves as subject of the verb *visited* in the subordinate clause and joins the subordinate clause to the independent clause.)
- The tree you cut down stood on the plaintiff's property. (The subordinating conjunction *that* is understood between *tree* and *you*. The dependent clause is *you cut down*.)

Clauses are also classified according to the grammatical function they perform—noun, adjective, adverb.

Noun Clause as Subject: *Whoever pays the bill* calls the tune. (The noun clause *Whoever pays the bill* is the subject of the verb *calls*.)

Noun Clause as Object: They believed *that the time had come for action*. (The object of the verb *believed* is the noun clause *that the time had come for action*.)

Adjective Clause: *The man* who vaulted the fence *was being chased*. (The noun *man* is modified by the adjective clause *who vaulted the fence*.)

Adverb Clause: She replied that she would go *when she was ready*.

CLICHÉ

(The verb *would go* is modified by the adverb clause *when she was ready*.)

CLICHÉ

See FIGURATIVE LANGUAGE.

COHERENCE

Coherence is the relationship between concepts. It may refer to the relationship between concepts within a sentence, between sentences, or between paragraphs. Lapses in coherence often occur because writers overlook a vital link in a piece they are writing. Such lapses typically occur because writers know their subjects so well that their minds skip ahead in the development. Effective outlines, complete down to the last item in the development of a main idea, can prevent gross lapses, for example, neglecting to cover a major portion of a topic. Because the outline for a short paper is typically rough, however, it may not include mention of all the minor elements the writer should cover. Careful revision, in which the writers act as disinterested readers of their own material, will uncover major oversights as well as omissions of lesser elements.

When writers have not thought through their arguments completely before beginning to write, they should not be surprised to find that their discussions prove incoherent to their readers. Typically, careless writers fall prey to logical fallacies. In the fallacy called *post hoc ergo propter hoc* ("after this, therefore because of this"), a writer suggests mistakenly that an event has resulted in another event merely because the first event occurred before the second event—the child took sick because he disobeyed his mother's warning to dress warmly. In *begging the question*, the writer assumes as a fact the very thing that the writer set out to prove—parallel lines will never meet because they are parallel. A *non sequitur* is a conclusion that does not follow from the stated premises—she is an only child and, of course, will be selfish all through her life.

COLLECTIVE NOUN

A collective noun is one that names a group of persons, objects, or acts. Depending on the sense intended, a collective noun may be treated as a singular or as a plural. Once the choice of number has been made, the writer must maintain that number. That is, once a collective noun is treated as singular in a sentence or larger unit, it must always be treated as singular; once a collective noun is treated as plural, it must continue to be treated as plural.

Correct The *majority* of the group *is* for the proposal, and *it* insists on *its* right. (The collective noun *majority* is treated as singular, so the pronoun *it* and the possessive adjective *its* are singular.)

Correct The *majority* of the group *are* for the proposal, and *they* insist on *their* right. (The collective noun *majority* is treated as plural, so the pronoun *they* and the possessive adjective *their* are plural.)

The distinction between the two sentences is that the writer of the first sentence was thinking of the *majority* as a bloc, a unit. The writer of the second sentence was thinking of the *majority* as comprising many individuals.

Both of the following sentences are correct:

- The team decided to walk off the field because *they* thought the umpire was being unfair to *them*.
- The team decided to walk off the field because *it* thought the umpire was being unfair to *it*.

A case can be made for both these constructions—the first writer thinks of the team as a number of individuals, while the second writer thinks of the team as a single unit. You must decide which of the two you prefer. Just remember that the next time you deal with such nouns as *group, family, team, audience, orchestra, cast,* or *number,* you must decide whether you intend a plural or a singular. From then on, stay with your choice.

COLLOQUIAL LANGUAGE

Colloquial language is the language we normally speak rather than the language we normally write. Informal English differs from formal English in that it is closer to colloquial usage. There is nothing wrong with using colloquial language, but the inappropriate use of colloquial language in general and formal writing presents problems. For example, *ain't* is a handy and widespread locution that is acceptable in colloquial English, and unacceptable in general and formal written English. So-called slang and substandard English abound in rich expressions that have their place in communication, the only restriction being that, as writers, we must always choose the right place and the right time for using slang or substandard English.

35

COLON

A colon (:) is used (1) to set off a series of words, phrases, or clauses from the rest of a sentence; (2) to introduce a restatement, explanation, or illustration of a statement made immediately before; (3) to introduce a quotation of more than five lines; (4) to introduce a quotation in a sentence when the quotation is not closely related to the sentence; (5) to follow the salutation in a formal letter; (6) to separate hours and minutes when numerals are used; (7) to separate parts of a proportion in a scientific expression; (8) to replace a comma plus a conjunction, or a semicolon, for stylistic purposes; and (9) to separate elements of a footnote or bibliographic entry.

1. Series Use a colon to set off a series from the preceding elements of a sentence.

- Andrea checked off the items of equipment she would need: hip boots, rod and reel, flies, and landing net.
- Please supply the following: color monitor, laser printer, and work station.

2. Explanation Use a colon to introduce an explanation, restatement, or illustration of a preceding statement.

- Several persons recommended her for the job because of her background: five years at Georgia Tech, three years in the Army Engineers, and four years with United Technologies. (*Background* is restated in detail.)
- After weighing the evidence for several days, the jury brought in the verdict: guilty of murder in the second degree. (*Verdict* is explained.)
- Most of us thought our instructor was showing signs of depression: protracted periods of indecisiveness, unusual spells of forgetfulness. and irregular class attendance. (*Depression* is illustrated.)

3. Long Quotation Use a colon to introduce a quotation of more than five printed lines.

While Samuel Butler was justly famous as a novelist, he was also an early biological theorist:

> Surely the theory that I have indicated above makes the reason plain why no organism can permanently outlive its experience of past lives. The death of a body such as the crayfish is due to the social condition becoming more

complex than there is memory of past experience to deal with. Hence social disruption, insubordination, and decay. The crayfish dies as the state dies, and all states that we have heard of die sooner or later. There are some savages who have not yet arrived at the conception that all things die sooner or later. —*Unconscious Memory,* p. 148.

4. Quotation Within a Sentence Use a colon when incorporating a quotation into a sentence if the quotation cannot be run in with a comma or without punctuation. The colon implies that the quotation is only loosely related to the sentence.

- In a preface to one of his lesser known works, he writes: "While a trifling success would much gratify, failure would not wholly discourage me from another effort." (The colon, in conjunction with the opening quotation mark, signals clearly that a quotation is about to begin. A comma in place of a colon before the quotation may result in misunderstanding. Read the sentence with a comma in place of the colon to see how this might occur.)

- In a preface to one of his lesser known works, he writes, "While a trifling success would much gratify, failure would not wholly discourage me from another effort." (The problem with using a comma after *he writes* is that there is also a comma before *he writes*. Use of commas before and after *he writes* might lead the reader to think for a moment that the person being quoted has also written the words preceding *he writes*. With a colon after *he writes*, the reader correctly recognizes that the colon signals the start of the quotation.

5. Salutation Use a colon after the salutation of a formal letter.

- Dear Professor:
- Dear Ms. McCarthy:
- Gentlemen:

6. Time Use a colon between hours and minutes in giving time.

- 12:30, 1:45

7. Proportions Use a colon in giving proportions.

- The fertilizer contained nitrogen and potash in the precise proportion 5:10.

8. Stylistic Reasons Use a colon when you desire a more complete break between independent clauses than is accomplished by use of a comma plus a conjunction, or in place of a semicolon.

- Citizens of a successful democracy should not only cast a vote: they should cast educated votes. (A semicolon would also be correct here.)
- There was only one possible way to deal with the situation: she tore off her shoes and plunged into the water after the drowning child. (A more complete break is needed here than would be achieved by use of a semicolon. A comma plus the conjunction *so*, for example, would not achieve the relationship indicated by use of a colon.)

9. Footnotes and Bibliography If you follow the bibliographic practice still employed in many journals, use a colon between the place of publication and the name of the publisher in a footnote or in a bibliographic entry. Although this practice is not followed any longer by most journals or by the authors of this book, it is included here because some editors and teachers still adhere to this practice. (For the recommended form of footnotes, see FOOTNOTES.)

- *Footnote* Austin Clarke, *Flight to Africa* (Dublin: Dolmen Press, 1963), p. 21.
- *Bibliographic Entry* Clarke, Austin. *Flight to Africa*. Dublin: Dolmen Press, 1963.

COMMA

The comma (,) is the most common mark of punctuation and the most commonly misused. Some of the blame for this misuse must rest with teachers of composition who lose patience with pupils struggling to learn all the intricacies of this troublesome mark—and why shouldn't students struggle? Punctuation is an unnatural act. The marks of punctuation appear only on the written or printed page, even though in recent years many people have fallen into the misguided habit of saying *quote/unquote* while they are talking and even go so far as to make quotation marks in the air with extended fingers while saying *quote/unquote*. If you look back at examples of English and American writing of a century or more ago, you will see that the practice of punctuation was much different then. Readers in earlier times were accustomed to a system of punctuation much more complex and more idiosyncratic than our own.

The rationale for using commas, as well as for using all the other marks of punctuation, is that properly used punctuation can help readers understand the intentions of a writer more readily than they can without it. The practice of inserting a comma wherever a reader might pause in reading a sentence aloud is not valid. This might work if we all breathed evenly.

The principal uses of the comma are: (1) to separate coordinate clauses, (2) to set off nonrestrictive clauses and phrases, (3) to set off introductory elements, (4) to set off parenthetic expressions, (5) to separate the elements of a series, (6) to separate coordinate adjectives, and (7) to set off miscellaneous expressions—dates, geographic entities, and units of counting.

1. Coordinate Clauses Use a comma and a coordinating conjunction between coordinate clauses—clauses of equal status in a sentence.

- The suspect entered the building, and the detective followed closely behind. (two independent clauses)
- Relative frequency of inadequate nutrition in childhood is important, but there are several other important factors that must be considered. (two independent clauses)
- The team members were eager to get to the soccer field by noontime, for the championship match was scheduled for two o'clock and would certainly attract a large number of spectators. (The second independent clause has a compound verb, *was scheduled* and *would attract*.)
- Our company must become serious about improving its minority employment practices, or it will certainly face federal court action. (two independent clauses)

If you cannot see that the use of commas in these sentences is important, consider the role the comma plays in each of the next examples:

- The famished wolf devoured the dying hare, and the pack of dogs ran away.
- Our birch tree quickly lost all its leaves, and the maple was not far behind.
- The firefighters played their hoses on the raging fire, and the police officers kept the crowds back.
- Debate in the General Assembly failed to convince most delegates that the problem demanded solution, and debate in the Security Council proved equally unconvincing.

Without a comma before the conjunction in each of these four examples, the reader might think that the wolf devoured the dying hare and the pack of dogs, that the birch tree lost all its leaves and the maple as well, that the firefighters played their hoses on the raging fire and the police officers, and that the problem demanded solution and debate in the Security Council. The comma between coordinate clauses in each of these sentences prevents even a moment's uncertainty.

2. Nonrestrictive Modifiers Use a pair of commas to separate nonrestrictive phrases and clauses from the rest of a sentence. If the phrase or clause introduces or terminates the sentence, use only one comma.

- Charles Dickens, *one of the most noted of English novelists*, was attracted to the deformed, the half-witted, and the abandoned. (Because *Charles Dickens* identifies the author sufficiently, the italicized phrase that follows is classified as nonrestrictive and therefore is enclosed in commas.)
- Dublin, *which has some of the most celebrated Georgian buildings in Europe*, is now strongly under the influence of modern architectural styles. (The same reasoning applies. In this case, a nonrestrictive clause is enclosed in commas.)
- Many consider the modern era in Mexico to have begun with the Mexican Revolution, *surely one example of a good use of force*. (The italicized phrase is nonrestrictive, since *Mexican Revolution* is sufficient to identify the historical event. Because the nonrestrictive phrase occurs at the end the sentence, only one comma is used.)
- *A man endowed with the virtue of humility*, President Coolidge avoided intervention and sent an emissary bent on arriving at a peaceful solution. (President Coolidge is President Coolidge. Identifying him as a man endowed with the virtue of humility does not serve to identify him. The nonrestrictive phrase is set off by a single comma because it occurs at the beginning of the sentence.)

3. Introductory Elements Use a comma to separate all clauses, verbal phrases, and prepositional phrases of more than three words that precede the main statement of a sentence.

- Since their original premises now seemed to be open to doubt, they laid aside the line of investigation and once more thought out the problem from the beginning. (*Since their original premises now seemed to be open to doubt* is a subordinate clause that is separated by a comma from the independent clause that follows.)

- In order that people may truly live rather than merely exist, they must have a reasonable income. (Same situation as in the preceding example. Subordinate clause: *In order that people may truly live rather than merely exist.*)

- Showing uncharacteristic modesty, many successful people deprecate their own achievements. (*Showing uncharacteristic modesty* is a verbal phrase that is separated by a comma from the independent clause that follows.)

- With hardly a trace of emotion, Inspector O'Byrne continued her investigation at the scene of the crash. (*With hardly a trace of emotion* is a prepositional phrase of more than three words. It is separated by a comma from the independent clause that follows.)

4. Parenthetic Expressions Use commas to separate parenthetic expressions from the rest of a sentence.

- The workers must, of course, have adequate leisure. (Parenthetic expression: *of course*. A pair of commas is needed.)

- Adequate leisure, to be sure, means time to pursue interests other than those connected with work. (Parenthetic expression: *to be sure*. A pair of commas is needed.)

5. Lists and Series Use a comma between unpunctuated elements in a series or list. If the elements of the series are internally punctuated, use a semicolon.

- The buyer selected three pins, two ties, a sweater, and a brooch from the fall line. (Commas will do the job, because there is no punctuation within elements.)

- They marched before the retiring Mayor in regular order: the Police Band first, then the Fire Band, and finally the Sanitation Fife and Drum Corps. (Commas again.)

- Mickey ordered cereal, which turned out to be indigestible; two slices of toast, neither of which had been near a toaster for at least an hour; and ham and eggs, which bore little resemblance to what he remembered of this dish in his mother's kitchen. (Commas between elements of the series will not do the job in this sentence. Since there already are commas within the elements, semicolons must be used.)

Some writers insist on omitting the comma normally preceding the *and* before the final element in a series. There is no adequate justification for this practice. Inserting this last comma, which may not always appear necessary, may sometimes prevent serious misunderstanding. A comma takes up little space and may preserve clarity.

- Their business was that of distributing milk, cheese, eggs, and butter. (Four elements in the series, with a comma before the *and* preceding the final element. While no harm would result from omitting that comma, see the following examples.)
- The family once operated a large and thriving enterprise in new construction, renovations and repairs, and kitchen cabinet design and installation. (The commas, including the final comma before *and kitchen cabinet design and installation*, make it clear that the enterprise had three major divisions.)
- All we heard from them were excuses, sweet talk, and hearts and flowers. (This series has three elements, the last of which is an expression meaning "maudlin sentimentality." *Hearts and flowers* would lose that meaning if a comma appeared after *hearts*. The comma before the final element in the series, *hearts and flowers*, makes it clear that *hearts and flowers* is to be understood as a unit.)

6. Coordinate Adjectives Use commas to separate two or more adjectives in a series if they modify a noun in the same manner.

- A *thick, solid* door stood under a deeply curved arch.

The adjectives *thick* and *solid* both modify *door* in the same manner—a *thick door*, a *solid door*—so they are classified as *coordinate adjectives*. Notice that the conjunction *and* can be used in place of the comma between these adjectives: A *thick and solid door stood under a deeply curved arch*. The comma between coordinate adjectives can always be replaced by *and*.

- The *hot, sticky, humid* air made everyone miserable.

Again, all three adjectives modify the noun in the same manner and are classified as coordinate. The word *and* can again be used instead of commas: hot *and* sticky *and* humid air. A practical test for determining whether adjectives are coordinate—and therefore must be separated by a comma—is to try substituting *and* between the adjectives. When *and* makes good sense, a comma is needed.

- An *old oaken* bucket lay beside the abandoned well.

There is no comma between the adjectives *old* and *oaken*, indicating that they are not coordinate. *Old* does not modify *bucket*. It modifies *oaken bucket*. Try placing *and* between the two adjectives: *An old and oaken bucket lay beside*…. Because *old and oaken* makes poor sense, the adjectives are not coordinate, and a comma may not be used between them.

7. Miscellaneous Uses Use a comma between the day of the month and the year; after the salutation in a personal letter; between city or county, and state; in numbers, to separate thousands, millions, etc.; with names in direct address; and after exclamations.

Dates June 29, 1992
March 4, 1948

British usage inverts the order of elements in a date and does not use commas: 29 June 1992; 4 March 1948. Modern American usage tends to omit the comma between month and year.

- December 1997.
- July 1821

Salutations in Personal Letters Dear Joan, Dear Mom,

Places Wilmington, Ohio
Suffern, Rockland County, New York
Numbers 25,480 1,399,467 221,000,000
Names in Direct Address John, I want to tell you a story.
Exclamations Gosh, that was a good game.
Oh, what a beautiful morning!

COMMA FAULT

Comma fault is the term teachers of composition employ to indicate mistakes of two types: (1) use of a comma to separate related independent clauses when a semicolon, colon, or period is needed, and (2) use of a comma between independent clauses in the absence of a coordinating conjunction. A writer whose sentence has been labeled *comma fault* must decide whether to replace a comma with a semicolon, colon, or period or to retain the comma and add a conjunction. Examine the following examples of comma faults and their revisions:

Comma Fault The Hemingway hero is a mystery, how did he start, where did he come from? (Commas—without connectives—are used between three independent clauses. Such punctuation is not ordinarily considered acceptable.)

Revised The Hemingway hero is a mystery. How did he start, and where did he come from? (The first independent clause has become a sentence. The second and third independent clauses are more closely related to one another than they are to the first independent clause. They have been connected by *and* plus a comma to form a second sentence.)

Revised How did the mystery of the Hemingway hero originate? (This is a more concise way to introduce the subject, but you can be certain that the discussion will go on to discuss *how* the Hemingway hero started and *where* the Hemingway hero came from.)

Comma Fault Four volumes of the work have been set in type, the first will be issued within two months. (A comma cannot do the job alone. The connective *and* is an obvious solution.)

Revised Four volumes of the work have been set in type; the first will be issued within two months. (Rather than use *and* plus a comma, the writer has chosen to use a semicolon, which does not require a connective.)

Comma Fault I believed that her advice was sound, nevertheless I acted on it with caution. (A comma is not considered adequate between clauses connected by *nevertheless*, *however*, *notwithstanding*, or any other CONJUNCTIVE ADVERB.)

Revised I believed that her advice was sound; nevertheless, I acted on it with caution. (In this correction of the comma fault, *nevertheless* now is correctly preceded by a semicolon and followed by a comma.)

Comma Fault All industrialized nations seeking to develop products based on advanced technology should first examine their educational systems thoroughly, they will soon realize that sophisticated manufacturing requires an ample supply of highly trained technicians. (A single comma tries but fails to connect two independent clauses.)

Revised All industrialized nations seeking to develop products based on advanced technology should first examine their educational systems thoroughly, for they will soon realize that sophisticated manufacturing requires an ample supply of highly trained technicians. (The solution chosen here is to supply the connective *for*. A semicolon without a connective would also do the job, but writers are advised against resorting too often to the use of semicolons. A plethora of semicolons makes for heavy going.)

Run-together sentences of the types shown are common in the writing of the young, but by the time students reach college, they should have overcome this fault. If you are prone to *comma faults*, carefully reread every sentence you write to see whether it is indeed a valid sentence. You will soon be rid of comma faults.

COMPARE, CONTRAST

Compare to is used to point out similarities, and the people or things being compared may sometimes be from the same or from different categories, or universes.

- The dean compared the errors in my paper to the errors in Kate's paper. (The dean was indicating that the errors were comparable. Both sets of errors are from the same universe, in this case student papers.)
- Shall I compare thee to a summer's day? (Shakespeare here was paying an extravagant compliment by pointing out the similarities between his loved one and a beautiful summer day in England. Obviously, a summer day and the beloved person who is being addressed are from different universes.)

Compare with is used in the sense of "examine," pointing out differences as well as similarities.

- The teacher compares my driving ability with my brother's. (The examiner is pointing out that our driving abilities are different as well as similar.)
- She compared Yeats's poetry with Blake's. (She showed how the work of these great poets was different and how it was similar.)

Contrast with is used to point out differences.

- The book contrasts the foreign policy of the Soviet Union with that of India. (We expect to be told of the differences between the foreign policies of these countries.)
- Education in the United States contrasts markedly with education in Japan. (Again, the emphasis is on the differences between the school systems in the two countries.)

COMPARISON OF MODIFIERS

Adjectives and adverbs, the two general types of modifiers, have comparative and superlative forms in addition to absolute forms. The comparative indicates differences in degree between two elements.

- Hazel is taller than Harry. (*Taller* is the comparative form of *tall*.)

- It is difficult to determine from census data which city has the larger population, Tokyo or New York. (*Larger* is the comparative form of *large*.)

The superlative indicates the difference in degree among three or more elements.

- Alfred is the tallest member of the family. (*Tallest* is the superlative form of *tall*.)
- It is often difficult to determine which city has the largest population, New York, Tokyo, or London. (*Largest* is the superlative form of *large*.)

In colloquial language, the superlative is often used when no specific comparison is intended.

- She is the greatest.
- You are the best.

With adjectives and adverbs of three or more syllables, the comparative and superlative are generally expressed by using *more* and *most* with the absolute form.

Absolute	Comparative	Superlative
beautiful	more beautiful	most beautiful
immediate	more immediate	most immediate

Many adjectives and adverbs can be compared either by adding *er* and *est* to the absolute or by using *more* and *most*.

Absolute	Comparative	Superlative
often	more often	most often
often	oftener	oftenest
kind	more kind	most kind
kind	kinder	kindest

The *er, est* form stresses the quality; *more* and *most* stress the degree of difference.

Some adjectives change form completely when moving from the absolute to the comparative and superlative.

Absolute	Comparative	Superlative
good	better	best
bad	worse	worst

COMPLEMENT

Complement is the name given an adjective or noun that follows—and completes, *complements*—a linking verb. An adjective acting as

complement is called a *predicate adjective*. A noun acting as complement is called a *predicate noun*. The name *complement* is derived
from a Latin word meaning *that which fills up*, and "fill up" is what a
complement does for an otherwise meaningless linking verb. After all,
one cannot *is* or *was* unless one *is* or *was* something.

- He was *handsome* in his youth. (Predicate adjective.)
- Dr. Murray was the *surgeon* in the case. (Predicate noun.)
- The dish tastes *delicious*. (Predicate adjective.)
- Ms. Hawkins will be someday be our only *lexicographer*.
  (Predicate noun.)
- As usual, the sophomores sounded *ridiculous*. (Predicate adjec-
  tive.)
- Our instructors always are *graduate students*. (Predicate noun
  phrase.)

In case you are wondering about Hamlet's "To be or not to be," it
is worth saying that Shakespeare intended that we understand *be* to
mean "exist" or "live."

On a more practical point, be certain not to confuse *complement*
and *compliment*. When used as a verb, *complement* means "complete." When used as a noun, *complement* means "that which completes." Whether used as a verb or noun, *compliment* means "praise."

COMPOUND PREDICATE

A compound predicate consists of two or more verbs having the
same subject—compound verbs—plus the rest of the PREDICATE.
Two compound verbs are not punctuated; three or more are punctuated as a series.

- The wind *lashed* the cliffs and *leveled* the trees. (Compound
  verbs. Compound predicate: *lashed the cliffs and leveled the
  trees*.)
- The wind *lashed* the cliffs, *leveled* the trees, and *tore* at the
  homes along the ridge. (Compound verbs. Compound predicate: *lashed the cliffs, leveled the trees, and tore at the homes
  along the ridge*.)

Compound predicates tighten up the structure of a sentence, pre-
venting so-called primer sentences, sentences that are overly simple.
Consider the following examples of primer sentences:

- The wind lashed the cliffs. It leveled the trees. It tore at the
  homes along the ridge.

COMPOUND SENTENCE

A compound sentence consists of two or more independent clauses. The principal difficulty with compound sentences is correct punctuation. A compound sentence may be punctuated with a comma followed by a coordinating conjunction, or by a semicolon, either alone or followed by a CONJUNCTIVE ADVERB.

Coordinating Conjunctions—examples: and, or, for, but, so, yet, nor, while—*Preceded by a Comma*

- He was certain he had left his keys somewhere in the house, *but* he could not find them.
- The spectators roared their approval, *and* the players continued to punch one another halfheartedly.
- Several centuries have elapsed since we were supposed to have emerged from the so-called Dark Ages, *yet* we do not seem to be any more tolerant of our fellow men and women than were our earliest ancestors.

The Semicolon, with or without a Conjunctive Adverb—examples: nevertheless, notwithstanding, thus, however, moreover, accordingly, furthermore, indeed—*in Compound Sentences*

- My classmates discussed the incident almost incessantly instead of paying attention to their studies; they talked of little else until the end of the term. (Semicolon without a conjunctive adverb.)
- It was Nature's fashion; she never quite reacts as we expect her to. (Semicolon without a conjunctive adverb. Notice that *Nature* is capitalized because it is personified. See PERSONIFICATION.)
- She relied exclusively on the darker tones in painting portraits; *moreover*, her subjects approved her work. (Semicolon plus conjunctive adverb: moreover. Comma after the conjunctive adverb.)
- The ambition of the Emperor was confined to the land; *nevertheless*, Augustus stationed two permanent fleets in the most convenient ports of Rome. (Semicolon plus conjunctive adverb: nevertheless. Comma after the conjunctive adverb.)
- But such was not the case; *indeed*, it has been pointed that transoceanic flights were impossible at that time. (Semicolon plus conjunctive adverb: indeed. Comma after the conjunctive adverb.)

COMPOUND SUBJECT

When a verb has more than one subject, the subject is classified as compound. The verb following a compound subject is plural unless both parts of the compound subject refer to the same thing.

- The ball and the bat *are* part of the Babe Ruth Collection. (Plural compound subject: *ball and bat*.)
- Truth and courage *are* no longer found in some departments of the executive branch of government unless the investigator is willing to search hard. (Plural compound subject: *Truth and courage*.)
- Detroit and its environs *are* known for *their* concentration of Americans of Polish descent. (Plural compound subject: *Detroit and its environs*. The verb *are* and the possessive adjective *their* are plural.)
- That the team had won and that it had won decisively *was* of no importance to him. (Singular compound subject: *That the team had won and that it had won decisively*. Both parts of the compound subject refer to the same thing.)

CONCRETE WORDS

Concrete words name things that can be seen and touched—head, hair, hedge, window, gas station, garage, and tens of thousands of other words. Concrete words are always preferable to abstract words, which designate acts, theories, ideas, qualities, relationships. Of course, one cannot use concrete words exclusively to describe abstractions. The mistake poor writers make is to use abstract words when the situation calls for the concrete. The result is sentences cluttered with words that may appear high-sounding, but actually are at least one step removed from telling a clear story.

CONDITIONAL CLAUSE

A conditional clause states the action or condition needed to establish the validity of the main statement of a sentence. The most common conjunction used with conditional clauses is *if,* but *if not, unless,* and *whether* are also used. Conditions may be classified as *practical* or as *contrary to fact*. This classification determines the MOOD of the verb in the conditional clause.

Practical conditions are those in which the main statement will be possible if the conditional statement is fulfilled.

CONDITIONAL CLAUSE

For practical conditions, use the simple form of the verb in the conditional statement and use the simple or future form in the main statement.

- If you *hear* the signal, *call* out. (Simple form of the verb in the conditional statement: *If you hear the signal*. Simple form in the main statement: *call out*.)
- If the plane *does* not *arrive* on time, we *will lose* our hotel reservations. (Simple form of the verb in the conditional statement: *If the plane does not arrive on time*. Future form in the main statement: *we will lose our hotel reservations*.)
- Unless we *honor* this important commitment, the Secretary said, our allies *will* not *believe* any of our other professions of commitment. (Simple form of the verb in the conditional statement: *Unless we honor this important commitment*. Future form in the main statement: *our allies will not believe any of our other professions of commitment*.)

Conditions contrary to fact are those in which the statement in the conditional clause is obviously not true and cannot become true. In formal expression, use the subjunctive mood in the conditional clause, the simple or future form in the main statement.

- If I *were* you, I *would walk* on the other side of the road. (I cannot be you, so the condition is contrary to fact and is expressed in the subjunctive mood: *If I were you*.)
- If she *be* the woman she claims to be, she *will* not *press* for payment under these circumstances. (The implication is clear: she is not the woman she claims to be. Therefore, the conditional clause employs the subjunctive mood: *If she be the woman she claims to be*. If the writer intended to suggest that she is the woman she claims to be, the verb would be in the indicative mood: *If she is....*)
- If we really *were* dishonest, we *would* not *behave* in that way. (Use of the subjunctive *were* suggests that we are not dishonest.)

Use of the subjunctive mood in conditions contrary to fact is dying out even in formal English, but it is still helpful in expressing fine shades of meaning. Consider the following pair of sentences:

- If he *be* the expert they say he is, he will surely see that the painting is not the work of Renoir.
- If he *is* the expert they say he is, he will surely see that the painting is not the work of Renoir.

The writer of the first sentence is certain that the man being discussed will prove to be anything but expert. The writer of the second sentence is willing to give the poor wretch a chance of showing that he is an expert. Again, when a candidate says, "If I *am* elected, I will not serve," he means that he may be elected and that he really will not serve. But when a man says, "If I *were* elected, I would not serve," he means that his chance of being elected is nonexistent. He gives up nothing by making this bold statement.

These distinctions between subjunctive and indicative moods add up to this consideration: Concern yourself with the problem of the correct form of the verb in a conditional clause when you are on your best behavior. When you are concerned with subtleties of expression, use the subjunctive mood to state conditions contrary to fact. This means using *were* or *be* instead of *was* in the first and third person singular.

- If I *were* king....
- If he *were* the last man on earth....
- "If this *be* treason, make the most of it."

CONJUNCTION

A conjunction is a word or group of words that joins words, phrases, or clauses. *Coordinating* conjunctions join clauses of equal weight—usually, independent clauses. *Subordinating* conjunctions introduce statements that describe or qualify a word or concept in the main clause.

The correct use of conjunctions is one sign of a mature writer, and care should be taken both in formal and informal writing to be certain that the most appropriate conjunctions are used. When we speak with another person, we can indicate a great deal concerning the relationships between concepts by the tone of our speech, by pauses, shrugs, and facial expressions. In writing we are deprived of these valuable tools, and a great deal of the burden of expressing our thoughts precisely must be carried by the conjunctions we use. The following sentences demonstrate some of the interpretations drawn by the writers of this book from the use of a few common conjunctions:

- The war will end *when* we stop bombing. (There is no certainty that we are contemplating cessation of bombing.)
- The war will end *if* we stop bombing. (The uncertainty has increased.)

- The war will end *whenever* we stop bombing. (We are in complete control. We can stop whenever we wish.)
- The war will end *even though* we stop bombing. (We see little reason for stopping.)
- The war will end *after* we stop bombing. (We appear to have decided to stop bombing at some time in the future.)
- The war will end *because* we stop bombing. (No one else has anything to say about when the war will end.)

CONJUNCTIVE ADVERB

Conjunctive adverbs are adverbs that can be used as conjunctions between independent clauses, for example: *accordingly*, *also*, *anyhow*, *besides*, *consequently*, *furthermore*, *hence*, *however*, *indeed*, *instead*, *likewise*, *meanwhile*, *moreover*, *namely*, *nevertheless*, *notwithstanding*, *otherwise*, *still*, *therefore*, *thus*. Such words can convey a good deal of information, so we must not hesitate to use them where appropriate.

Yet, conjunctive adverbs carry a penalty: they require additional punctuation—a semicolon before a conjunctive adverb and a comma after the conjunctive adverb. For this reason we use conjunctive adverbs only when necessary, and as a rule only in formal writing. Poor writers tend to rely too heavily on conjunctive adverbs, making their prose ponderous. Many engineering and scientific journals offer multiple examples of excessive reliance on these conjunctions.

Consider the following pair of sentences, both of which are correct:

- Editors can improve a manuscript, *but* they cannot easily supply essential thoughts that are not already present. (One comma, one conjunction—meaning clear.)
- Editors can improve a manuscript; *however*, they cannot easily supply essential thoughts that are not already present. (One semicolon, one comma, one conjunctive adverb—little added to meaning by using *however* instead of *but*.)

The choice a writer makes between these sentences is based on the intent of the writer, not on grammatical correctness. *However* performs much the same function as that performed by *but*. Yet, *however* does affect the meaning of the sentence in a way slightly different from the way *but* affects that meaning.

- The Senator tried her best to push the modified bill through, *but* she was not able to get it out of committee. (One comma, one conjunction—meaning clear.)

- The Senator tried her best to push the modified bill through; *nevertheless*, she was not able to get it out of committee. (One semicolon, one comma, one conjunctive adverb—little added to meaning by using *nevertheless* instead of *but*.)

Now try the following sentence:

- We were assured that we had done everything that could be done for the sick man: we responded promptly, administered all indicated drugs, and introduced intravenously all prescribed fluids; *thus*, we were certain there would be no recriminations from anyone in a position of authority.

This sentence presents a great deal of information and does so in a necessarily complex sentence. The conjunctive adverb *thus* provides an appropriate transition to the final thought of the sentence. An ordinary conjunction would not serve well here. Try replacing *thus* with *and*, *so*, or *but*. The first two conjunctions would make good sense but would not capture the idea of "as a result of all this" that is conveyed by *thus*. The third conjunction, *but*, would convey an erroneous impression. Notice too that some of the other conjunctive adverbs listed in the first paragraph of this entry would also do the job performed by *thus*, but care must be taken in choosing among them. *Consequently*, *hence*, and *therefore* would be acceptable.

Whenever you complete a draft of a paper, check all your sentences to see how many conjunctive adverbs you have used. Have you *thussed*, *howevered*, *therefored*, and *punctuated* your reader into a state of disbelief or revulsion?

This discussion has centered on the punctuation of conjunctive adverbs that are used to connect independent clauses. Conjunctive adverbs also are used, however, before independent clauses and within independent clauses. When conjunctive adverbs are used in these ways, commas alone provide sufficient punctuation. Consider the following examples:

- *However*, the council agrees that nothing is served by remaining intransigent.
- The council agrees, *however*, that nothing is served by remaining intransigent.

These sentences have only one independent clause, *The council agrees*. In both sentences, the conjunctive adverb *however* provides a connection to a sentence (not shown here) occurring immediately before the sentence. When a conjunctive adverb is used to open a sentence, as in the first example, it is set off by a single comma. When the conjunctive adverb is placed within a sentence, as in the second example, it is set off by a pair of commas.

Notice too that *however* and some other conjunctive adverbs may be used as simple adverbs:

- *However* hard you try, you may fail. (*However* modifies *hard*.)
- Handicapped *thus*, the swimmer could not complete the race. (*Thus* modifies *handicapped*.)

CONTACT CLAUSE

Contact clauses are two or more coordinate clauses that stand together with a comma between them. Such clauses are more characteristic of narrative writing than of expository writing, but when used intentionally as a stylistic device, they are appropriate in formal as well as informal writing. For student writers and developing writers, what appears to be a pair of contact clauses frequently turns out to be a COMMA FAULT. The distinction between contact clauses and a comma fault is difficult to determine, so most teachers and many editors are inclined to regard the use of contact clauses as poor style. There is no rule that tells when and when not to use contact clauses. One bit of advice is never to use them in a freshman composition course. A more serious suggestion is to use contact clauses only when the clauses are brief and closely related in meaning.

- Speak up, you will probably be right.
- Enunciate clearly, make certain you can be heard.
- Eat little, live long.

CONTRACTION

Contractions are words from which unstressed syllables have been omitted—*won't, isn't*. Since contractions are common in conversation, most dialogue uses them. Contractions are also used in informal and general English, but not in formal English. Consider the audience for whom you are writing when you are about to use a contraction.

COORDINATING CONJUNCTION

A coordinating conjunction is used to join two grammatical elements of identical construction—words, phrases, or clauses. The most common coordinating conjunction used to join words and phrases is *and*. The principal coordinating conjunctions used to join independent clauses are *and*, *but*, *for*, *nor*, *or*, *while*, *yet*, and *so*. When one of these conjunctions is used to join independent clauses, it is preceded by a comma.

- The month of November drew slowly to a close, *and* the boys were satisfied with the continuing mild weather. (The coordinating conjunction joins two independent clauses.)
- Many of this year's class of adult students cannot even write simple sentences, *but* their instructors are determined to do everything they can to help the students achieve satisfactory proficiency in composition. (The coordinating conjunction joins two independent clauses.)
- Little remains to be done in completing the project, *so* most of the volunteers have decided to go home. (The coordinating conjunction joins two independent clauses.)

Compound constructions, for example, compound subjects and compound predicates, should not be punctuated unless they are exceptionally long or complicated.

- The theater *was closed and completely redecorated* once the season was over. (No punctuation within the compound construction *was closed and completely redecorated*, because the construction is relatively short and straightforward.)
- Despite all our efforts, there was nothing *to do but abandon* the search. (Same comment.)
- Professor Schmidt *reviewed* the academic background and scholarly accomplishments of all the candidates for the position, and *agreed* that only two of them were worthy of further consideration. (Because the compound construction *reviewed and agreed* is relatively long and complicated, a comma is used after *position* to help comprehension.)
- The aerodynamic design was *noteworthy* in several respects but *deficient* in others, and so was returned to the design team for further refinement. (Same reason for using a comma after *others*.)

CORRELATIVE CONJUNCTION

Correlative conjunctions are used in pairs with grammatically similar constructions. Although purists insist that both such constructions be exactly parallel, some shifts are common—particularly in informal writing. The principal correlative conjunctions are *either ... or, not only ... but also, neither ... nor,* and *whether ... or.*

- *Either* you go *or* I go.
- *Not only* was Carol a good student, *but* she was *also* well liked by her classmates.
- *Neither* you *nor* your friend may stay late.
- *Whether* Jill walks *or* runs, she is always in a hurry.

D

DANGLING MODIFIER

A dangling modifier is a modifier that appears to modify a word it cannot reasonably relate to—the modifier has been misplaced. When you discover such an error in style, you must usually recast the entire sentence. There are two ways to do this. Either place the modifier as close as possible to the word or construction it modifies, or supply a word or construction that can be modified properly.

Incorrect Dashing through the room at top speed, the door obstructed her. (*Dashing through the room* is classified as a dangling modifier. Doors cannot dash through a room.)

Correct As she dashed through the room, the door obstructed her exit. (Dangling modifier removed. People can dash through a room.)

Incorrect To wield it properly, the handle must be grasped firmly. (We have no idea of what *it* refers to, so *To wield it properly* is a dangling modifier. The sentence appearing before this sentence may have provided the explanation, or it may not have. At any rate, considering this sentence alone, it looks as though we wish to wield a handle. Surely there must be more to it than that.)

Correct To wield an axe properly, the handle must be grasped firmly. (Now we know what is to be wielded. The dangling modifier has been eliminated.)

Correct To wield an axe properly, one must grasp its handle firmly.

Incorrect He was arraigned for filching fresh fish in Felony Court. (Did he filch the fresh fish in Felony Court, or did he filch it elsewhere? Surely he must have been arraigned in Felony Court for filching fresh fish elsewhere.)

Correct He was arraigned in Felony Court for filching fresh fish.

In most cases, dangling modifiers do not confuse the reader. Relying on context clues, the reader is well aware (a) that a woman is dashing through the room, (b) that it is a tool of some kind that must be wielded, and (c) that the fish-filching did not occur in Felony Court. Yet Murphy's First Law of Writing threatens: *Anything that can be misunderstood will be misunderstood.*

Is there any chance whatsoever that confusion can result from a dangling construction? If there is, the construction must be avoided.

Is extra effort required of readers to understand what a writer is trying to say? Reading is difficult enough without making the process unnecessarily difficult. Is there any chance that a construction can be interpreted in a way that holds the writer up to ridicule? Careful editing can elminate such constructions. (See also SPLIT VERB FORMS.)

DASH

The dash (—) is used (1) to indicate a sharp turn in thought, (2) to set off a summary statement, and (3) to enclose parenthetic statements when the writer wishes to give them more stress than they would receive if they were enclosed in commas.

Sharp Turn in Thought
- Helene was motivated by a love for power—not freedom—and she set out to acquire as much power as she dared.
- The general effect of the book—to call it by a more exalted name than it really deserves—is to pitch readers alternately into sardonic groans and fits of derisive laughter.

Summary Statement
- The courtly senator was all that constitutes a gentleman—in carriage, gait, address, gesture, voice, courtesy, and self-assurance. (The summary statement precedes the specific listing of attributes.)
- The last farewells, the bumpy ride to the airport, the interminable wait at the ticket counter, the embarrassing baggage security inspection—all that was over, and they were off on their honeymoon. (The summary statement follows the list of specific details.)

Parenthetic Statement
- Many subjects—sociology and anthropology, for example—interested him enough to make him want to remain on campus for another year.
- The polished manners and elegance of dress—acquired in society—are by society admired.

Many writers appear frightened by the dash, suggesting that they are uncertain of its proper use and its appropriateness in general writing. The dash should be thought of as a mark that emphasizes sentence elements that do not occupy emphatic positions. If used sparingly for that purpose, the dash is effective. To use the dash in the way teenagers may use it in letters to a best friend—often as the only mark of punctuation in their letters—is to rob the dash of its ability to heighten and clarify.

DEADWOOD

Deadwood is the term used by teachers to characterize writing they consider to be too full of meaningless words, phrases, and sentences. Elimination of this stylistic error calls for unrelenting use of the red pencil during every revision to strike out anything that does not contribute to meaning. In the deadwood forests of much student writing, the most prominent specimens are strings of adjectives and adverbs that can be eliminated if suitable nouns and verbs are used. Another rich harvest is possible if every sentence within a paragraph is examined for unnecessary repetition of identical ideas and information, albeit expressed differently. Entire sentences may disappear as a result of such careful reading.

In dealing with the problem, ask yourself what each sentence really says and whether its meaning is (1) different from what the rest of the paragraph says and (2) useful in the development of the paragraph. If sentences do not meet these two tests, strike them out.

DECLENSION

Declension is the inflection of nouns and pronouns to indicate gender, number, and case. English has no declension worth mentioning in comparison with the declension of Latin, German, or Greek. English nouns have only two forms to show differences in function (*case*)—the common form and the possessive. Pronouns have three cases—subjective, objective, and possessive—but the declension is not regular.

Lack of declension is one indication of the maturity of the English language as well as a partial explanation of why the grammar of English is so difficult for native and foreign students alike.

DELETE

Delete is the command used by teachers and editors to signify that they are thoroughly displeased with the content or quality of the writing before them. They may abbreviate delete as *dele*, as the Greek lower case delta (∂), or as a line drawn through the offending material. Frequent application of *delete* to your papers should alert you to the need for more rigorous editing on your part before submitting future papers. (See DEADWOOD.)

DEMONSTRATIVES

Demonstratives are adjectives and pronouns that indicate, or single out, other words. (Many students of grammar fail to distinguish between demonstrative adjectives and demonstrative pronouns. An adjective modifies. A pronoun stands in place of a noun, performing many of the same functions. In the sentence "That hurts," *That* is a pronoun functioning as subject of a verb, *hurts*. In the sentence "That book is mine," *That* is an adjective functioning as a modifier of a noun, *book*.)

- *This* hat looks as good to me *this* year as it did last year. (Two demonstrative adjectives. The first indicates *hat*, the second *year*.)
- *Those* cadets never seem to tire of parading back and forth. (Demonstrative adjective indicating *cadets*.)
- *This* is the best I have read so far. (Demonstrative pronoun indicating a book, poem, paper, or some other written matter.)
- *These* are the items my aunt left us in her will. (Demonstrative pronoun indicating certain personal possessions.)

DICTION

Diction refers to the words we use in speaking and writing. The term is often used as a teacher's comment on themes to call attention to faulty use of words, suggesting that the misuse can cause misunderstanding by readers or inadequate appreciation of the writer's intent. It goes without saying that words must be chosen carefully if we are to write effectively. Student writers who are habitually careless or often off the mark in choosing words will help remedy faulty diction by becoming devotees of the dictionary and thesaurus. This practice—finding words in a thesaurus and then making certain of their meanings by checking the words in a dictionary—combined with a systematic program of vocabulary enrichment, will eventually cure problems of diction. This is not to say that the best words are rare or elegant. Everyday words can effectively describe most of our thoughts. The problem is one of choosing the right word, not the fanciest.

DISINTERESTED, UNINTERESTED

Disinterested and *uninterested* represent just one among many losing battles that have been fought over the generations by purists—self-appointed guardians of purity in usage. Writers for many years restricted use of *disinterested* to the meaning "objective" or "impartial." At the same time they used *uninterested* to mean "having no interest in" or "bored." Alas, current usage no longer supports this distinction. Most often today, except in the writing of highly educated people, *disinterested* is used interchangeably with *uninterested* to mean "having no interest in" or "bored." Indeed, when *disinterested* is used to mean "objective" or "impartial," many people will stare at the person using *disinterested* in this way. Unfortunately for those who wish to retain the "objective or impartial" meaning exclusively, there is plenty of evidence showing that as far back as the 17th century *disinterested* has meant "having no interest in."

All this is not intended to ask you to follow current usage in regard to *disinterested* and *uninterested*. Teachers and editors will be pleased if you use *disinterested* in the "objective or impartial" sense. As educated people they expect that judges of prize fights and horse races, as well as judges sitting in our courts, should always be disinterested in carrying out their professional duties. Heaven forbid that they ever become uninterested!

DIVISION OF WORDS

There are widely accepted rules governing the division of words in a manuscript, but most publishers and teachers prefer a jagged right-hand margin with few, if any, divided words to a right-hand margin that is even but full of divided words. This relieves the printer or the teacher of the job of wondering whether the writer intends a hyphenated word or a divided word.

Some general rules for dividing words are helpful. (1) Never divide a word when only one letter will be left on a line. (2) It is always permissible to divide a word between double consonants. (3) Both divided parts should be pronounceable. (4) Never divide words of one syllable.

DOUBLING FINAL CONSONANTS

The most useful spelling rules in English concern the doubling of a final consonant before adding a suffix. These rules have no—repeat no—exceptions, which is why they are so useful. Although the rules may appear complicated, they are worth committing to memory.

Words of One Syllable

In words of one syllable ending in a single consonant preceded by a single vowel, double the final consonant before adding a suffix beginning with a vowel.

- bat: batted, batting, batty
- sin: sinner, sinning (but sinful)
- run: runner, running, runny

All three words—*bat*, *sin*, *run*—have one syllable. Each ends in a single consonant. The final consonant is preceded by a single vowel. The only one of these three words in which the final consonant is not doubled when adding a suffix is *sinful*. Why? Because the suffix added is *ful*, which begins with a consonant.

Words ending in a double consonant retain the double consonant when followed by a suffix beginning with a vowel. Such words may lose a final consonant when followed by a suffix beginning with a consonant.

- will: willed, willing, willful (*also* wilful)
- skill: skilled, skillful (*also* skilful)

Modern American usage prefers retention of the double consonant when followed by a suffix beginning with a consonant, as in *willful* and *skillful*.

Words of More Than One Syllable

In words of more than one syllable ending in a single consonant preceded by a single vowel, double the final consonant before adding a suffix beginning with a vowel *if* the accent in the original word is on the final syllable and adding the suffix does not cause the accent to shift.

- refer: referred, referring (but *referee, reference*)
- confer: conferred, conferring (but *conferee, conference*)

Both *refer* and *confer* have two syllables and end in a single consonant that is preceded by a single vowel. The accent in both words is on the final syllable. The first suffixes that were added to both words were *ed* and *ing*. Addition of these suffixes does not cause the accents to shift. Thus, the final *r* doubles: *referred, referring; conferred, conferring*. When *ee* or *ence* is added, the accents shift away from their original locations: *re fer EE* and *RE fer ence, con fer EE* and *CON fer ence*. The final consonants, therefore, are not doubled.

Wherever you encounter an apparent exception to any parts of the rule stated for doubling final consonants, check first to see whether all parts of the rule obtain. *Transferable—transfer* plus *able*—is not an exception, because the accent has shifted from *trans FER* to *TRANS fer a ble*. *Excellent* is not an exception because the accent has shifted from *ex CEL* to *EX cel lent*. And so it goes. Learn this spelling rule even if you never learn another.

DUE TO

Opinion is divided and vocal on the propriety of using the prepositional phrase *due to*. Purists insist that *due*, originally an adjective, should not be used in a prepositional phrase. They insist that *owing to* or *because of* should be substituted. According to recent studies, however, *due to* is used in over half the situations in which any of the three expressions could have occurred. It seems unlikely that this trend can be stopped by the opposition of teachers, editors, or writers of books on style. We might point out that *due to* does not appear to be as resolute as *because of* or *owing to* and that *due to* looks as though it may be more at home in bank statements than in English sentences.

E

EACH

Although *each* is singular, it carries an indication of plurality (*each of them*). This indication of plurality causes problems in the reference of pronouns and in the number assigned to verbs.

Formal Each of the performers carried out *his* task perfectly.
Each of the principals fulfilled *her* assigned responsibility.
Informal Each of the performers carried out *their* tasks perfectly.
Each of the principals fulfilled *their* assigned responsibilities.
Formal Each of these problems *is* an aspect of a larger problem.

Remember that most of the articles and papers you will write are formal papers, so take care not to be lulled into carelessness by the apparent anarchy of current popular practice. Stay on the safe side.

ED

Teachers who concern themselves with proper diction constantly find themselves restoring dropped *eds*, and many editors have inserted their share of *eds* in copy being prepared for publication. The problem arises partly because many past forms ending in *d* have tended to be pronounced as *t*, as in *patched quilt* (patch quilt). Again, words ending in *d* before a word beginning with the letter *t* often have both sounds assimilated into one: *in regard to* may be pronounced *[in regar ə]*, and *in respect to* becomes *[in respec tə]*. While such assimilation may sometimes be acceptable in speech, it should not be reflected in the spelling of these words. The past tense and the past participle of regular verbs end in *ed*. Only in dialogue can these letters be omitted.

When certain nouns function as adjectives, locutions have arisen in which the omission of *ed* is accepted: *ice cream* for *iced cream, whip cream* for *whipped cream, frame house* for *framed house, post free* for *posted free, pickle relish* for *pickled relish, one hundred room mansion* for *one hundred roomed mansion, patch quilt* for *patched quilt.*

EI, IE

The old rule—now practically as well known as the Pledge of Allegiance—holds that "*i* comes before *e* except after *c*." Instead of going on to repeat all the words that give us exceptions to this rule, learn to add, "but *e* after *i* when the sound is *[ā]*.'"''

- achieve, believe, friend
- deign, eight, weight

But there is the exception *seize*. Remember it.

EITHER

Used as a pronoun, *either* is singular. When acting as the antecedent of another pronoun or possessive adjective, *either* is still treated as singular.

- Either *is* all right.
- Either the tractor or the car *is* always in need of repair.
- Either of the students *is* qualified for graduate school.
- Either of the students is able to explain *his* position on the matter satisfactorily.
- Either of the students is able to explain *her* position on the matter satisfactorily.
- Either of the newspapers is going to have to redefine *its* position if *it* wants to retain respect.

ELLIPSIS

Ellipsis (... or ....) indicates that a word or more has been omitted from a quotation. When three points (...) are used, the reader knows that the omitted material does not include the end of a sentence. When four points (....) are used, the reader knows that the omitted material is from the end of a sentence or that more than one sentence has been omitted.

> They are ... dramas of thought, not of action.... He makes the character under dissection explain itself. In some cases deliberately, and in others consciously, it reveals its very inmost soul....
> —Ester Defries, *A Browning Primer*

Three points can also be used in dialogue to indicate a pause in speech, but this mark is rare in student papers. Above all, do not use more than four points and never use points to imply anything unstated. The so-called pregnant pause should be left to the correspondence of young lovers.

EMPHASIS

One way to give emphasis to your most important thoughts in writing is to assign them positions that naturally endow words with emphasis. Generally, the two most emphatic positions in a paper, paragraph, or sentence are the beginning and the end. In a paper, this means that the subject should be introduced in the opening of the paper and repeated in other words in the closing. In a paragraph, the topic sentence should come first or last, depending on the paragraph structure desired. In a sentence, the subject and verb are the most emphatic elements. The most important thoughts of a sentence should be carried by the subject and verb, and these cornerstones of the sentence should ordinarily be placed close to the beginning of the sentence.

Emphasis can also be achieved by using clear and precise language and avoiding unnecessary words, which usually rob a thought of emphasis. This does not mean that words can never be repeated nor that thoughts can never be repeated. (Notice the repetition of *can never be repeated*.) Deliberate repetition adds emphasis, and even beginning writers can use this device effectively to make certain the reader grasps the message. But this repetition is never done well if it is done carelessly. When repetition results from carelessness, the trivial may be repeated as often as the important is repeated.

EUPHEMISM

A euphemism is an expression used in place of a stronger expression that is generally unacceptable in formal English or in place of an expression that is considered offensive.

Government officials lay much store in euphemisms. For example, economic statistics are often couched in euphemistic terms by officials seeking to avoid giving the public any bad news. The words "depression" and "crash" are avoided by these officials. Instead, "slowdown," "downturn," even "negative economic growth" will be used. Pentagon officials avoid "killing" and "death," preferring instead to speak of "casualties" and other words that mask the grim truth. For example, when troops have died as the result of accidental explosions caused by negligence of United States forces, it is reported that the troops were "exposed to friendly fire."

For many generations, euphemisms have been employed to dance gingerly around topics that may offend. The topic most apt to offend sensibilities has long been anything dealing with sexual activity. In the King James Version, the translators used the verb "know" rather than "have sexual intercourse," which is one of the current euphemisms for the act—see how difficult it is even now to come up with a socially acceptable verb. Prostitutes and prostitution inevitably give people trouble. Today we may say "call girl" rather than "prostitute," and writers in the past often spoke of "women of easy virtue," "women of ill repute,"and "loose women." Eugene O'Neill had one of his characters in *Ah, Wilderness!* say "whited sepulchre" instead of prostitute. The word "prostitute" itself is a euphemism for "whore," a term that has been in our language for about a thousand years but still is not used in polite company.

O'Neill's expression was entirely in keeping with the social scene described in the play, but what of the rest of us? Under the pressure of the work of modern writers—as well as the linguistic lapses of respected public officials who are heard speaking unguardedly on television—many euphemisms are disappearing. Still, euphemisms persist in much formal and general writing, and we are well advised to consider the feelings of the people for whom we write. (See GOBBLEDEGOOK.)

EXCLAMATION POINT

The exclamation point (!) is used after a forceful interjection or after an exclamatory phrase, clause, or sentence. Use the exclamation point sparingly. Excessive use is like crying wolf too often. And never—*repeat never*—use more than one exclamation point at a time. !!! is no more expressive than !, and ! will not cause teachers and editors to squirm.

EXPOSITORY WRITING

Expository writing is writing that is intended primarily to inform. This characteristic sets limits on the nature of paragraph development and on the choice of language and stylistic constructions. Nonfiction prose is generally expository, and almost all writing done in college, except for creative writing, is expository.

F

FARTHER, FURTHER

No distinction is made between *farther* and *further* in general writing, but in formal writing *farther* refers to distance, and *further* refers to abstract concepts.

- The village lies twenty miles *farther* downstream than my map indicates.
- Guided missiles employed in the present conflict are designed to travel much *farther* than artillery shells and still strike targets with great accuracy.
- We must inform you that *further* discussion is impossible as long as you remain obdurate.
- If you go any *further* with this kind of behavior, you will soon be in trouble with the authorities.

In general writing *further* would probably be used in all four sentences, although some books, newspapers, and magazines would use *farther*.

At the same time, only *further* is used in the sense of "additional." This is the meaning intended in the sentence "We must inform you that further discussion is impossible...."

FIGURATIVE LANGUAGE

Language can be literal or figurative. Literal language means just what it says. Figurative language is metaphoric.

- In colonial times hunters *skinned* animals they killed and used the pelts to make clothing and shelters. (An example of the literal use of the word *skinned*.)
- Some Wall Street traders *skinned* their clients mercilessly before adequate regulations were put in place to prevent this. (An example of the figurative use of *skinned*.)

When writers use figurative language, they are borrowing terms that are literal in one context and using them in a context in which they become figurative. Thus, some of us may say that a professional baseball player "has swung his bat and hit the ball." That is literally what has happened. A sportswriter for a daily newspaper, desperate at having to describe the same action again and again every day for six months, might write:

- The batter cut at a jug-handle curve and rocketed it into the grandstand.

This kind of writing relies for its descriptive power on figurative language. After all, the batter does not intend to *cut* the ball literally, nor does the curve have a *jug handle*—only jugs do. And no matter how hard a batter manages to swing, one cannot say literally that he has *rocketed* the ball.

Figurative language is appropriate and desirable when it is fresh and adds power or character to writing. Figurative language is inappropriate when it is stale, worn out, hackneyed—choose the term you like best. Needless to say, most attempts at figurative language by mediocre sportswriters end in disaster.

What may once have been a sparkling metaphor in the hands of the exceptional writer may eventually become a cliché. In your own writing, avoid any figure of speech you have heard or read. Try to be original even though you know you sometimes will fail. Surely, however, you must never describe anyone as *pure as the driven snow* nor will you ever be guilty of offering your readers *out of the mouths of babes*, *in the nick of time*, *a fate worse than death*, or *a miss is as good as a mile*.

FINITE VERB

A finite verb is a verb that is limited in person (first, second, or third); in number (singular or plural); or in tense (present, past, or future). Verb forms that are not so limited are termed *infinite*: the infinitive (*run, have run*—also given as *to run* and *to have run*) and the participle (*running, run*).

FOOTNOTES AND BIBLIOGRAPHY

Whenever a writer uses material from a published source—whether the writer is quoting directly or is paraphrasing—that use must be recognized, either within the text or in a footnote, and in a bibliographic entry. The footnote must supply the author's full name, title of the work, place and date of publication, and the page number:

- [1] Compton Mackenzie, *Carnival* (London, 1912), p. 159.
- [2] C.S. Lewis, "On Obstinacy in Belief," *Servance Review,* LXIII (Autumn, 1955), p. 527.

Within the text the footnote number should be placed at the end of the material quoted and above the line, thus.[3]

FOR

The bibliography is an alphabetical list of the works cited in the footnotes, with the author's last name given first:

- Lewis, C.S. "On Obstinacy in Belief," *Servance Review*, LXIII (Autumn, 1955), 525–538.
- Mackenzie, Compton, *Carnival*. London 1912.

FOR

For serves both as a conjunction and a preposition. When *for* is used as a conjunction, it is preceded by a comma.

- Evelyn was eager to leave, *for* the dance was dreary and the hall cold and dark. (Two independent clauses connected by the conjunction *for*, which is preceded by a comma.)
- Jon thinks we ought to serve dinner early, *for* no one wants to stay out late on a weeknight. (Same comment.)

When *for* is used as a preposition, it usually is not preceded by a comma, but a comma may be needed for another reason. Each instance, therefore, must be judged individually. When in doubt, check the rules for the uses of the COMMA.

- Both drama clubs decided to buy presents *for* their coaches. (Preposition *for*, no comma needed.)
- Some attack dogs are trained to go *for* a person's leg. (Same comment.)

FOREIGN TERMS IN ENGLISH

The frequent use of foreign words and expressions in English writing reflects one of the ways that our language develops—linguists recognize that ancient languages and all modern languages tend to augment their word stocks in the same way. The English language is still growing vigorously, so the practice of borrowing from other languages goes on unchecked—indeed, it may even be accelerating—and foreign borrowing from English is occurring at an even dizzier pace.

The great majority of foreign terms in English have been assimilated; that is, they have been part of English for so long that their foreign origins are not obvious to most people. Consider such words as chauffeur, chassis, chivalry, garage, honor, kowtow, and shibboleth. These are just a few of the many hundreds of thousands of words of foreign origin that have long been accepted as English, not to mention the thousands of borrowings that—often with only slight changes in spelling—formed the nucleus of the earliest form of the language called English.

Some terms of foreign origin, while longtime members in good standing of the English language, are recognized readily as having come from foreign sources, for example, adios, eureka, faux pas, hoi polloi, and kimono.

Other terms of foreign origin in English have been with us for a short time and we readily recognize their foreign origins. Consider bagel, ersatz, falafel, pita, pizza, raison d'être, and tête-à-tête. It is conceivable that the two examples given last will one day lose their accents, because that is what normally happens when foreign terms become part of English, but raison d'être and tête-à-tête still retain their accents.

Other words, however, appear in English writing and speech but have not yet been assimilated, for example, *intifada*, *shalom*, *tant pis*, and *Weltschmerz*. Some writers think that a sprinkling of foreign terms can dress up a paper or article, marking the writer as a superior stylist. It does not. Foreign words should be used in English writing when (1) the context makes foreign words appropriate or (2) when satisfactory English equivalents for foreign words cannot be found. Thus, when writing dialogue in which readers expect to encounter the occasional Hebrew word, *shalom* may be appropriate, but there is no reason for writing *shalom* when "hello" or "good-bye" is appropriate, just as— unless the context calls for using a French expression—there is no reason for writing *tant pis* when "so much the worse" will do. *Weltschmerz* and *intifada* are examples of foreign words so specialized in meaning that they have no completely satisfactory English equivalent.

Two practical points to remember: (1) When a foreign expression is used, the word or words are underscored (italicized) in formal writing, but practice is divided in general writing. Consult a current unabridged English dictionary when in doubt. (2) Foreign words that have not been fully assimilated retain their accents, and German nouns are capitalized, since that is the practice in German style: *Weltanschauung*, *Lebensraum*. Again, consult a recent unabridged dictionary for guidance.

FORMAL ENGLISH

Formal English is the level of expression appropriate to formal writing and speech. When we mix words from one level of usage— formal, general, colloquial—with another, we may end up with unsatisfactory expression. It is true, however, that many words are appropriate to all levels of usage.

Consider this sentence, in which words from formal English seem out of place because most of the sentence is cast in general language:

- To an extraordinary degree, Hemingway and the books he wrote exist in a *synergetic* relationship, reinforcing and fulfilling each other; Hemingway has a personal legend that serves as an *ambiance* in which we read his work.

The student who wrote this ugly sentence has obviously found in the work of literary critics a pair of words that appealed to the student's undeveloped sense of style, unaware that they do not seem at home in the student's writing. *Synergetic* and *ambiance*—ugh!

FORTUITOUS, FORTUNATE

Fortuitous, the first of this pair of words, was defined formerly only in the sense of "happening by chance" or "unplanned." Recently, however, it has been used over and over again to convey the sense of "marked by luck," which indicates that it has become a synonym for *fortunate*. While we may abhor the linguistic phenomenon of robbing a word of its historic meaning, we must recognize that the confusion of *fortuitous* and *fortunate* is but one more example among thousands of examples of popular usage triumphing over careful usage. (See DISINTERESTED, UNINTERESTED.)

Despite what others may do, you would do well in your own writing to restrict use of *fortuitous* to the sense of "happening by chance."

- The fatal accident, you may be certain, was entirely *fortuitous*. (No fatal accident can ever be considered fortunate.)

FRAGMENTARY SENTENCE

A fragmentary sentence is one that lacks a subject or a verb or does not express a complete thought. Many excellent modern writers deliberately use fragments with great effect. But, as with so many aspects of style, the beginning writer should avoid fragments. In college papers, fragmentary sentences are taken to be the result of carelessness. Such sentences may add little to the development of a thought and add much to the discomfort of teacher and critic.

The most frequently encountered fragments are subordinate clauses or phrases treated as complete sentences; in most cases they should be joined to the preceding sentence.

Undesirable Fragment He walked for three hours in the hot sun. Because his car had run out of gas.

Complete Sentence He walked for three hours in the hot sun after his car had run out of gas.

Undesirable Fragment She was anxious about the interview. Apparently not being certain of her qualifications for the position.

Complete Sentence Because she was uncertain of her qualifications for the position, she was anxious about the interview.

Just because good modern writers occasionally employ the fragment, do not feel that you will suddenly reach a point in your development as a writer when your teachers will join you at tea and announce that from then on you will be entitled to use fragments whenever you wish. Most good modern writers never use fragments at all but go on publishing.

G

GENDER

There are three genders in English: masculine, feminine, and neuter. Fortunately, writers do not have to concern themselves much with gender. On the other hand, the Romance languages, among others, are loaded with problems of gender that plague the struggling student.

Gender in English is indicated for most words by the use of pronouns (*his*, *hers*, *its*) or by the use of certain suffixes (author*ess*, host-*ess*, avia*trix*). Such feminine endings now are eschewed by many female practitioners (imagine a women's liberationist writer referring to herself as an authoress!) and will probably disappear from the language before too long. It is unlikely, however, that we will ever lose such useful terms as goose and gander, fox and vixen, bull and cow, rooster and hen, and lord and lady.

Most inanimate objects are referred to in the neuter, but ships and the moon remain feminine.

GENITIVE CASE

The genitive (possessive) case is the form of nouns and pronouns that shows possession. There are four ways to show possession in English:

1. The most common is the addition of an apostrophe and an *s* to a singular noun and to certain plural nouns.

- girl's book, England's rivers, King's Inn, a man's hat, a woman's cloak, one hour's delay
- men's concerns, women's issues

Words ending in *s* take an apostrophe alone or an apostrophe plus a second *s* if the combination is not displeasing.

- Euripides' plays, Yeats's poems

Plural nouns ending in *s* take the apostrophe alone.

- boys' clothing, nuns' habits, three weeks' holiday

2. Possession can also be shown by using a prepositional phrase beginning with *of*.

- the valley of the Boyne, the poetry of Yeats, the plays of Arthur Miller

3. Possessive adjectives show possession.

- my book, our book, your book, his book, her book, its paws, their books

(See number 4 immediately.)

4. Personal pronouns can be inflected to show possession.

- mine, ours, yours, his, hers, theirs

Personal pronouns function as pronouns; possessive adjectives function as adjectives.

- *Mine* is missing. (Personal pronoun functioning as subject of verb.)
- *My* purse is missing. (Possessive adjective modifying noun.)
- *Hers* probably will prove to be the correct solution. (Personal pronoun functioning as subject of verb.)
- Who can see any merit in *his* point of view? (Possessive adjective modifying *point of view*.)
- They failed to see any merit in *his*. (Personal pronoun functioning as object of preposition.)
- We never will forget *their* courtesy. (Possessive adjective modifying noun.)
- The judges will surely find *theirs* the best entry in the show. (Personal pronoun functioning as object of verb.)

5. Possession can be indicated by a double genitive, combining the *of* construction with the possessive form. This form is often used to prevent ambiguity.

- *that picture of Eileen's* (Writers of phrases such as this one are intent on making it clear that they are referring to a picture *by* Eileen rather than *of* her. To say *Eileen's picture* may imply a portrait of Eileen or a picture drawn by her. The double genitive avoids this ambiguity.)

GERUND

A gerund is a VERBAL. A gerund looks like a present participle, in that it is the *ing* form of the verb, but a gerund functions as a *noun*, while the present participle functions as an *adjective*. (See PARTICIPLES.)

Gerund *Fishing* was his favorite sport. (*Fishing* is the subject of the verb.)

Much to her surprise, she found *fishing* exciting. (*Fishing* is the object of the verb.)

Present Participle *Fishing* up and down the river, he was a sight to behold. (*Fishing* is the modifier of *he*.)

Because a gerund is a verbal, it may be modified by an adjective or an adverb. It may also take an object and may perform any noun function.

- *Occasional reading* does not satisfy him. (Gerund *reading* modified by adjective *occasional*.)
- *Light entertaining* is common in the United States. (Gerund *entertaining* modified by adjective *light*.)
- They gave themselves over to *watching* television during the tense days of the war in the Middle East. (Gerund *watching* acting as object of preposition *to*. The same gerund itself takes an object, *television*.)
- *Reading continually* enabled him to maintain a degree of composure. (Gerund *reading* modified by adverb *continually*.)
- They enjoyed *entertaining*. (Gerund *entertaining* acting as object of verb *enjoyed*.)
- *Entertaining* his guests *afforded* him much pleasure. (Gerund *entertaining* acting as subject of verb *afforded*.)
- By *satisfying* her *clients*, she improved her prospects of promotion. (Gerund *satisfying* with object of gerund *clients*.)

A gerund, like an infinitive, which is also a verbal, can indicate tense and voice.

Active *Visiting* ancient villages on the Continent always gives them great pleasure. (present)

Passive *Being seen* in trendy restaurants interests more people than you would expect. (present)

Active *Having read* the book was achievement enough, he explained. (past)

Passive *Having been seen* near the scene of the crime was what disturbed him most of all. (past)

Subject of the Gerund

A gerund may take a subject. When that subject is a pronoun, the pronoun must be in the objective case.

- They found *Edward lying* on the floor. (The gerund *lying* has *Edward* as subject.)
- They found *him lying* on the floor. (The pronoun *him* serves as subject of the gerund *lying* and is, therefore, in the objective case.)

Case of Gerund Modifiers

In formal writing, the possessive case is used for gerund modifiers.

- Sean did not mind *my going*. (The modifier of the gerund *going* is *my*, a possessive adjective.)

- Nobody showed concern over *his leaving* before the dinner was concluded. (The modifier of the gerund *leaving* is the possessive adjective *his*.)
- In view of the circumstances, I did not object to *Henry's performing* so badly. (The modifier of the gerund *performing* is *Henry's*, the possessive form of *Henry*.)

If the modifier has no possessive form or is in the plural, the possessive is not used.

- The teachers hoped that the parents who agreed to serve as chaperons on the field trip would not interfere too much in the *mountain climbing*. (*Mountain*, the modifier of the gerund *climbing*, has no possessive form.)
- Can you conceive of the *intelligentsia deciding* to remain silent after the Nobel Prize was awarded to so popular a novelist? (*Intelligentsia* is a plural noun used to modify the gerund *deciding*.)

GET

The past participle of *get* is *got*, but *gotten* is also used in the present and past perfect and in informal English.

- What have you *got* (*gotten*) by those methods?
- He had *got* (*gotten*) past his final examinations and was ready for graduation.

GOBBLEDEGOOK (also given as Gobbledygook)

Gobbledegook is a term that describes euphemistic writing that goes around and around indefinitely, relying on fine-sounding terminology to confuse rather than enlighten the reader. Gobbledegook originally referred to bureaucratic jargon, but now it is in common use to cover all kinds of circumlocution.

George Orwell, in his essay "Politics and the English Language," cites a fictitious English professor who wants to justify Soviet totalitarianism. A simple statement of his position would be: "I believe in killing off your opponents when you can get good results by doing so." Unwilling, or congenitally unable, to make this straightforward statement, he writes instead:

> While freely conceding that the Soviet regime exhibits certain features which the humanitarian may be inclined to deplore, we must, I think, agree that a certain curtailment of the right to political opposition is an unavoidable concomitant of transitional periods, and that the rigors which the Russian people have

been called upon to undergo have been amply justified in the sphere of concrete achievement.

Such expression, as we all know, is all too common. Read any official statement by any group, or any profession of beliefs by a political candidate, and you will be rewarded with a fresh supply of gobbledegook. If you want to make up your own circuitous phrases, use the following lists of words. For a custom-made phrase that will amuse and impress—and say nothing—select one word at random from each column:

Column A	*Column B*	*Column C*
pragmatic	preternatural	ambiance
incremental	salutary	dichotomy
syncretistic	exophthalmic	megalomania
recondite	cooperative	expertise
homologous	simplistic	rationale
ambivalent	ontogenetic	*modus operandi*
charismatic	demagogic	covenant
de facto	epicene	atrophy
medieval	vertiginous	paradigm
didactic	holistic	parameter
a priori	ephemeral	symmetry

For your serious writing, develop an alarm system that will prevent you from resorting to gobbledegook. The simple statement is always the clearest. (See EUPHEMISM.)

H

HANG

The past participle of *hang* in the sense of "execute" is *hanged*. In other senses it is *hung*.

- The men were *hanged* in the public square.
- Most artists have *hung* their own paintings in our show.
- The side of beef has *hung* long enough.

HE, SHE

Speakers and writers of English wanting to refer to members of both sexes rather than one or the other sex are faced with the problem of REFERENCE when they must use the personal pronouns *he* and *she* or the possessive adjectives *his* and *her*. In the past it was common to use *he* and *his* even when a girl or a woman was understood to be included in the noun antecedent.

- Every *soldier* is responsible for keeping *his* barracks clean at all times. (This sentence attempts to impress on the reader that each soldier bears responsibility for the appearance of the entire barracks. Since the noun *soldier* now may include women as well as men, however, the possessive adjective *his* is unacceptable. The best way to remedy this problem is to cast sentences like this in the plural.)
- All *soldiers* are individually responsible for keeping *their* barracks clean at all times. (Even though the antecedent *soldiers* and the possessive adjective *their* are plural, the idea of personal responsibility is maintained by use of the adverb *individually*.)

Another possible solution calls for repeating a noun instead of using a pronoun to replace the noun.

- A good *manager* makes certain that all machinery used by members of the *manager's* staff is given all the care necessary to maintain it in good working order at all times. (The writer resists the temptation to write *his* or *her* instead of *manager's*.)

The problem of what has been termed *sexist language* pervades careless writing, so it is worthwhile to study a few more problem sentences and suggested corrections.

Poor Practice He announced that each employee would have to make *his* report in person. (This form was used commonly despite the fact that some of the employees were women.)

Suggested Change He announced that all employees would have to make *their* reports in person.

The announcement was made that reports would have to be supplied personally by each employee. (This sentence has no pronouns.)

Above all, in trying to avoid sexist language, do not resort to the clumsy *his or her, his and her,* or *his/her.*

Poor Practice The manager announced that each employee would have to make *his or her* report in person.

Despite the fact that profits were falling, they gave each employee *his/her* promised raise.

Suggested Change The manager announced that all *employees* would have to make *their* reports in person.

Despite falling profits, the manager gave all employees *their* promised raises.

Despite falling profits, all employees still received *their* promised raises.

HOMONYM

Homonyms, sometimes called homophones, are words that are pronounced alike but have different meanings and may have different spellings: *air* (gas) and *air* (melody) and *air* (ventilate); *air* and *heir*; *bear* and *bare, boar* and *bore, brake* and *break, fair* and *fare, feet* and *feat, him* and *hymn, mail* and *male.*

Homographs are words that are spelled alike but have different meanings—often different origins—and may be pronounced differently: *bear* (carry) and *bear* (animal), *lead* (metal) and *lead* (conduct), *row* (dispute) and *row* (straight line), *wind* (movement of air) and *wind* (twist).

HOWEVER

However is used as an adverb, a conjunctive adverb, and a parenthetic word. As an adverb, *however* can modify any number of adjectives: *however resolute, however numerous, however strong,* and many more. As a conjunctive adverb, *however* is most appropriate in formal English; in general English, it is usually replaced by *but* or much less frequently by a semicolon. As a parenthetic word, *however* is used to help make a pair of sentences more coherent.

- *However* ingenious they are, they will not be able to find a way out. (*However*, an adverb, modifies the adjective *ingenious*.)
- They were willing to accept all the honors that came with the appointment; *however*, they were not willing to do any of the necessary work. (The conjunctive adverb *however* can be replaced by the conjunction *but*, and the change will require only a comma before *but* instead of the semicolon. Needless to say, the comma used after *however* as a conjunctive adverb will be removed.)
- Several of the sheep made straight for the far corner of the field. One, *however*, veered off and had to be turned by the collie. (*However* here is used as an interruptive to improve the coherence of the two sentences.)

Writers are using *however* more and more frequently to form a bridge between two consecutive sentences. Consider again one of the examples given above: *They were willing to accept all the honors that came with the appointment;* however, *they were not willing to do any of the necessary work.* Writers now appear to be more comfortable with two sentences rather than one: *They were willing to accept all the honors that came with the appointment.* However, *they were not willing to do any of the necessary work.* Be warned that many teachers and editors show little enthusiasm for this use of a conjunctive adverb.

HYPHEN

The hyphen (-) is the mark that indicates the division of words at the end of a line of type or manuscript, splices words together to form compounds, and separates vowels when certain prefixes are added to words that begin with a vowel.

Word Division

Most teachers and printers would rather read pages of manuscript that have jagged right-hand margins than wonder whether the writer intended to end a line neatly by dividing a word or whether the writer thought good spelling required a hyphen. When you must divide a word at the end of a line, a hyphen is required.

- Divide between double consonants.
- Divide between syllables as long as both parts of the words are pronounceable.
- Never divide when only one letter will be left on a line.
- Never divide a word of one syllable.

Compound Words

Many English words pass through three stages in their development. They begin as two or more separate words. They then become hyphenated words. Finally, they become established as single, unhyphenated words. For example, the names of almost all ball games once were separate words: *foot ball*, *base ball*, and *basket ball*. They soon were spelled *foot-ball*, *base-ball*, and *basket-ball* before they reached their modern forms: *football*, *baseball*, and *basketball*.

Many words have stopped at the second stage of development and retain their hyphens—especially when the first part of the word is not a simple modifier of the other: *Anglo-American*, *secretary-treasurer*. When you are not certain of whether a hyphen is needed for a compound word, follow the lead of a good recent dictionary. Since hyphens have a way of disappearing over time, an old dictionary may not prove reliable.

Numbers and Modifiers

A hyphen divides numbers from *twenty-one* to *ninety-nine*; compounds of self, as in *self-knowledge* and *self-centered*; family relationships, as in *mother-in-law*, *daughter-in-law*, and *sister-in-law*; and two-word adjectives.

- *second-class* citizen, *tourist-class* cabin

A hyphen is used with a numeral that is part of a modifier.

- *6-foot* boards, *10-inch* beams

A hyphen is used with a letter linked to a noun.

- *X-ray*, *I-beam*

A hyphen is used with many adverb-adjective modifiers when the adverb does not end in *ly*.

- *well-traveled* road, *slow-moving* people, *late-blooming* plants
- *easy-going* person (now usually given as *easygoing* person)

The hyphen is dropped when the modifier is in the predicate position.

- Route 87 is *well traveled*.
- She cannot abide an assistant who is *slow moving*.
- This lettuce is *late blooming*.

When a group of words is intended as a unit, hyphens are usually required.

- *devil-may-care* attitude, *out-and-out* fabrication

But *nevertheless*, *heretofore*, *insofar*, and many other words made of separate words are considered single, unhyphenated words. (Check your dictionary when you intend to use a group of words thought of as a unit.)

Prefixes

To avoid ambiguities in pronunciation, as when two vowels are brought together by adding a prefix, a hyphen may be used:

- *semi-abstract, semi-industrialized, semi-intoxicated*

The hyphen has disappeared from a great number of words that were formed by adding the prefix *re* to a word beginning with the letter *e*, and from words formed by adding the prefix *co* to a word beginning with the letter *o*.

Modern Spelling reenter, reexamine, cooperate, coordinate
Older Spelling re-enter, re-examine, co-operate, co-ordinate

While the older spellings still are seen, editors and teachers consider that readers will have no difficulty with the modern spellings.

The hyphen is retained in words that would cause confusion with other words if the hyphens were omitted. Consider the following pairs: *recreation* (amusement) and *re-creation* (creating anew), *recollect* (remember) and *re-collect* (collect again). Because such pairs have entirely distinct meanings, the hyphens play an important role and therefore are retained.

The hyphen is used with stressed prefixes, such as *ex* and *all*.

- ex-Governor, ex-wife
- all-American, all-Conference

The hyphen is the most bedeviling of all the marks of punctuation. Since hyphens are used relatively infrequently and have a variety of uses, few writers can remember all words that should be hyphenated. If you use a dictionary as your authority on questions of hyphenation, be sure to use one and only one up-to-date dictionary—dictionaries do not all give the same guidance in spelling difficult words. By following the best dictionary you can find, you will achieve consistency of hyphenation. Another authoritative source is worth mentioning for serious writers. In any dispute over hyphens, you can rely on the *United States Government Printing Office Style Manual*, which devotes over fifty pages to punctuation and is generally considered by American writers to be The Last Word.

I

IDIOMS

An idiom is an expression whose meaning is different from the literal interpretation of the words that make up the full expression.

- The orchestra played the symphony sluggishly until the final movement, when it *caught fire* and *brought the house down*. (Can you imagine the reaction of a foreign reader who does not know these idioms?)
- The enemy forces were *caught with their pants down*. (The literal meaning of this idiom *boggles the mind*.)

All languages have their idioms. When the French, for example, want to express a thought that is relatively simple, they may employ idioms that can drive a young American student to distraction.

Idioms are important writing tools, but they lose their freshness when they are overworked. When they do, they are *old hat* (a cliché) and *should be dropped* from formal writing, along with *caught fire*, *brought the house down*, and *caught with their pants down*.

IF

If is a subordinating conjunction that introduces a condition.

- He will get the job *if* he applies immediately.
- *If* the food is good, a restaurant usually will prosper.
- All the trees offered for sale will thrive in this climate, *if* we can believe the mail-order catalogues that daily arrive at our door.
- *If* you can keep your head about you....

Whether, another subordinating conjunction, is used in place of *if* in expressing doubt and in phrasing indirect questions. *Whether* often appears in combination with *or*, but *if* is not used with *or* in formal English:

- He does not know *whether* he will go *or* stay. (formal)
- He does not know *if* he will go *or* stay. (informal)
- We cannot tell *whether* we are correct *or* not. (formal)
- We cannot tell *if* we are correct *or* not. (informal)
- We cannot tell *whether* we are correct. (formal and informal)
- We cannot tell *if* we are correct. (poor usage)

IMAGERY

Imagery in language is a word or group of words that appeals to the senses. Most poetry and much prose use imagery constantly to heighten meaning by appealing to the senses, supplementing the purely intellectual appeal of exposition. Yeats's "bee-loud glade" appeals to sound, sight, touch, smell, and—because we associate bees with honey—taste.

Writers should use imagery, but only if the images are fresh. Poor writers will often attempt to decorate their prose by resorting to what inevitably are poor images, invented by others and long ago discarded as trite. Your images should come from your own experience. In the famous passage below, which appears in *Walden*, see how Thoreau uses images from common experience. There is nothing exotic that he could not have experienced himself—at least secondhand, in the case of the reference to Sparta.

> I wanted to live deep and suck out all the marrow of life, to live so sturdily and Spartan-like as to put to rout all that was not life, to cut a broad swath and shave close, to drive life into a corner, and reduce it to its lowest terms, and, if it proved to be mean, why then to get the whole and genuine meanness of it, and publish its meanness to the world....

IMPLY, INFER

The confusion between *imply* and *infer* has almost become a national joke as the airwaves and the printed page become more and more cluttered by the efforts of word destroyers. But this is not the only pair of words that has suffered. DISINTERESTED and *uninterested* have gone the same way. The ability to keep these two pairs separate functions as a caste mark today.

The initiator *implies*, the receiver *infers*. Thus, the writer and the speaker will *imply*, and the reader and listener will *infer*. In the general language, as implied above, the distinction between these two words no longer exists. In all your formal writing and speech, be sure to observe the difference in meaning.

INDICATIVE MOOD

The indicative mood is the usual form of English verbs encountered in most clauses and sentences. The indicative makes an assertion or asks a question.

- The streets through which the procession *went were lined* with spectators who *watched* with delight. (Three indicatives: *went* in a subordinate clause, *were lined* in the independent clause, and *watched* in a second subordinate clause. All make statements.)
- Why *have* you *found* it necessary to cheat? (The indicative asks a question.)
- Where *will* we *be* one hundred years from now? (Again, an indicative used to pose a question.)

Some grammarians mistakenly assert that the indicative mood is used to state facts. Many a lie has been told in the indicative mood.

- The coalition *assured* us that there *would be* no punishment for deserters. (Two verbs in the indicative mood. Two lies: the act of assuring and the assertion that there would be no punishment for deserters.)

INDIRECT DISCOURSE

In indirect discourse, we paraphrase or summarize in our own words the writing or speech of someone else. In theme and report writing, indirect discourse saves space and time and usually represents an improvement in style compared with verbatim quotation.

Direct According to the Associated Press, "The crowds that lined the streets were inclined to behave well. There was much noise from horns, cowbells, frying pans, firecrackers, etc., but no serious disorder."

Indirect The Associated Press reported that orderly crowds lined the streets, and though they made much noise, no serious disorder occurred.

Direct The Texas Governor concluded her inaugural address by saying: "Finally, I want to thank all of you who worked so hard on behalf of my candidacy. I hope I will do nothing to disappoint you, and if for any reason you feel even slightly disappointed with my performance of the duties of the great office to which you have seen fit to elect me, please feel free to write me. I will respond quickly to right any injustice of which I may be guilty." (While the Governor's statement was worth reporting, it did not merit direct quotation.)

Indirect The Texas Governor concluded her inaugural address by thanking her supporters, pledging to do her best, and promising to hear and act on any complaint raised by her constituents.

Whether you quote or paraphrase depends on the language of the original and on your purpose in introducing the material. If you can paraphrase in fewer words than the original and not distort the tone or intent, then paraphrase. If the original is written especially beautifully or strikingly, and if the full quotation is useful to your exposition, then quote. Of course, even though indirect discourse does not employ quotation marks, you must nevertheless cite the source.

INFINITIVE

The infinitive is the unbounded root form of the verb, the form found in dictionaries. An infinitive is usually preceded by *to*, which is often called the sign of the infinitive: *to sit, to walk, to run*. An infinitive may not be readily identifiable when it appears without *to*. While absence of *to* does not affect the uses of infinitives, it may trouble a student who is attempting to analyze a sentence.

- You really helped them *to learn*. (infinitive with *to*)
- You really helped them *learn*. (infinitive without *to*)
- Dare *to be* different. (infinitive with *to*)
- Do you dare *come* without them? (infinitive without *to*)

Voice and Tense

Infinitives (see VERBAL) can have active or passive voice and simple or progressive tense:

	Active		*Passive*
	Simple	*Progressive*	
Present	to walk	to be walking	to be walked
Perfect	to have walked	to have been walking	to have been walked

The present infinitive indicates time that is the same as the time of the main verb or future to it.

- It is always pleasant *to walk* with you. (present tense, active voice)
- The leader of the opposition is willing *to hear* from you. (present tense, active voice)
- The President's secretary will be able *to see* you tomorrow. (present tense, active voice)

The perfect infinitive indicates time that is previous to the time of the main verb.

- I was happy *to have walked* with you. (perfect tense, active voice)
- Many clues seem *to have been removed* before we arrived. (perfect tense, passive voice)

Infinitive of Linking Verb

Usage is divided over the case of a pronoun after the infinitive of a linking verb. In general English, the objective case is used; in formal English, the subjective case is used.

General I supposed it to be *him.* (objective case after infinitive *to be*)

Formal I supposed it to be *he.* (subjective case after pronoun *to be*)

Infinitive in Absolute Construction

The infinitive can be used in absolute constructions.

- *To lead* the armed forces in the offensive, all units were put under unified command.
- *To ensure* achievement of high quality, inspectors observe every step in production.

INFORMAL ENGLISH

Informal English—the level of language we use in narrative, in informal talks, and in some social conversation—is rarely appropriate in general or formal writing. The interspersal of informal English within general or formal discourse is conspicuous because it clashes with the main body of expression. Such lack of consistency is poor style. If you need to find a general or formal expression to replace an informal expression, use your thesaurus and your dictionary.

IT

It is the neuter third person singular pronoun. When *it* functions as a pronoun with a clearly recognizable antecedent, *it* presents no problems. *It* does present a stylistic problem in the common constructions *it is* and *it was*. Examine the following sentences:

- *It was* in his hours of writing that he found peace and comfort.
- *It is* in evenings spent with her family that she finds greatest relief from the pressures of the business day.

In both these sentences, emphasis is lost by having the logical subjects *he* and *she* buried as subjects of the subordinate *that* clauses:

that he found peace and comfort and *that she finds greatest relief from the pressures of the business day*. What is more, the constructions *it was* and *it is* occupy the normal position of *subject* and *verb* in the main clause. But *it was* and *it is* by themselves say nothing. They merely provide a way to start a sentence or clause.

Unless the writers are striving for some rhythmic effect, the sentences should be:

- He found peace and comfort in his hours of writing.
- She finds greatest relief from the pressures of the business day in evenings spent with her family.

It was and *it is* have been removed, and the subject and verb of each sentence no longer are buried. They appear in their logical and prominent positions up front in the sentences: *He found...* and *She finds....*

Examine your writing for *it is, it was, there is, there are* constructions. How many of them can you justify? When you cannot point to a good reason for keeping them, cut them out and rewrite.

ITS, IT'S

Its is the possessive form of an adjective based on the pronoun *it*. The possessive does not have an apostrophe.

- Seven of *its* offspring went on to win major show awards. (Possessive adjective *its*. The *offspring* belong to *it*.)
- He wants to be sure that the house retains *its* scrubbed appearance until a receptive buyer is found. (Possessive adjective *its*. The *appearance* belongs to *it*.)
- I find *its* dog-eared pages annoying. (Possessive adjective *its*, referring to a book mentioned in an earlier sentence, not given here.)

It's is the contraction of *it is* and must have an apostrophe.

- *It's* a long, long way to Tipperary. (*It is*.)
- *It's* bound to be a difficult interview even if *it's* successful. (*It is, it is*.)

IT'S I, IT'S ME

The disagreement over whether to say *it's I* or *it's me* has its roots in the problem of which case to use when a pronoun serves as the complement of a linking verb. In formal English, the subjective case is used: *It is I; It was I.* In general English, usage is divided. In speech, almost all of us say *it's me* and *it was me*, and most grammarians accept these forms. Similarly, we say *it is him* and *it was him* rather than the formal *it is he* and *it was he*.

In most writing, the formal *it is I*, *it is he*, and the like are preferred. Ask yourself whether formal language is appropriate for a piece you are writing, and proceed accordingly.

J

JARGON

Jargon is highly specialized language peculiar to a trade or profession. Jargon is also a term applied to misuse of language. In this definition, jargon is marked by substitution of abstract words for concrete words; overuse of long, rare, and specialized words; and habitual reliance on words that are thought to be appealing but do not actually contribute to meaning.

Jargon is avoided in writing and speech by careful practitioners of a profession and by people expert in rhetoric.

K

KIND OF, SORT OF

In these locutions, *kind* and *sort* agree in number with the object of the preposition *of* that follows. When a demonstrative adjective—*that*, *this*, *these*, *those*—precedes *kind* or *kinds* and *sort* or *sorts*, the adjective must also agree in number.

- *That kind* of treatment by male colleagues persisted throughout her career. (*Treatment*, the object of the preposition *of*, is singular, so the demonstrative adjective *that* and the noun *kind* are both singular.)
- *This kind* of biscuit sells well throughout England. (*Biscuit*, the object of the preposition *of*, is singular, so the demonstrative adjective *this* and the noun *kind* are both singular.)
- *These kinds* of products sell poorly in my country. (*Products*, the object of the preposition *of*, is plural, so the demonstrative adjective *these* and the noun *kinds* are both plural.)
- *This sort* of foolishness must stop. (*Foolishness*, the object of the preposition *of*, is singular, so the demonstrative adjective *this* and the noun *sort* are both singular.)
- *Those sorts* of fellows always make enemies wherever they go. (*Fellows*, the object of the preposition *of*, is plural, so the demonstrative adjective *these* and the noun *sorts* are both plural.)

Mistakes such as *these kind of laws* and *those kind of people* mark the user as a poorly educated person.

KIND OF A, SORT OF A

Avoid *kind of a* and *sort of a* in formal writing. Although these constructions are frequently heard, they are not acceptable in formal or informal writing.

Some of us may say:

- He was that *kind of a* person.

But all of us should write:

- He was that *kind of* person.

L

LAY, LIE

Lay is a transitive verb, which means that it can take an object. *Lie* is an intransitive verb, which means that it cannot take an object, since no action is transmitted from the subject.

- If you are tired, why don't you *lay* down your load? (*Lay* is a transitive verb; the object of *lay* is *load*.)
- If you are tired, why don't you *lie* down? (*Lie* is an intransitive verb; it cannot have an object.)

The principal parts of the two verbs—the forms from which all tenses are formed: infinitive, past tense, past participle—are worth examining.

- *lay, laid, laid* (transitive)
- *lie, lay, lain* (intransitive)

These verbs give us trouble because the past tense of *lie* is *lay*, and writers may confuse *lay* in the past with the infinitive form *lay*.

Lay. I must *lay* my head on my pillow. (place it there)
She suddenly *laid* her cards on the table. (put them down)
He has *laid* his plans carefully. (developed them)
Lie. My golf ball *lies* just above the cup. (rests there)
Sabrina's book still *lay* where she put it yesterday. (remained there)
The homeless woman has *lain* there unnoticed all day. (been there)

You will find it worthwhile to memorize *lay, laid, laid* (transitive); *lie, lay, lain* (intransitive).

LEARN, TEACH

In nonstandard English, *learn* is sometimes used in place of *teach,* but in all other forms of English these two verbs have quite different meanings. Teachers *teach*; students *learn*.

- Jody *learned* more about mathematics in that one afternoon than he had been able to grasp in all his years of study until then. (*Learn* means "understand" or "grasp.")
- His father *taught* him to harrow the land carefully before planting. (*Teach* means "instruct.")

LEAVE, LET

Leave is often used in nonstandard English in place of *let* in the sense of "allow," "permit," or "release." Most teachers and editors consider this substitution incorrect in standard English. It therefore has no place in formal writing or speech.

Nonstandard Leave me go. (*Permit* me to go.)
Standard Let me go. (*Permit* me to go.)
Nonstandard Leave him escape. (*Allow* him to escape.)
Standard Let him escape. (*Allow* him to escape.)
Nonstandard Leave go of me. (*Release* me.)
Standard Let go of me. (*Release* me.)

LESS, FEW

Less is used for objects measured (amount), *few* for objects counted (number).

- Many people have urged that the mass media put *less* emphasis on violence. (We can *measure* emphasis; we cannot *count* it.)
- The recipe calls for *less* sugar than I anticipated. (We can only *measure* sugar; if we are foolish we may try to count grains of sugar.)
- Our project requires *few* tools. (We can *count* tools.)
- *Few* people are aware of all the preparations necessary before a Broadway performance. (We can *count* people.)

You may find it helpful to remember that *less* is an antonym of *more*, and *few* is an antonym of *many*: *less effort, more effort; few soldiers, many soldiers*.

LEVEL

Level (of diction) is a term frequently used by teachers to indicate that a word or phrase so marked is inappropriate in its context. A more appropriate word or phrase should be substituted. When in doubt about the acceptability of a word in general or formal writing, consult an up-to-date dictionary.

LIKE, AS

Grammarians seem to be fighting a losing battle in their effort to maintain distinctions between the functions of *like* and *as*. Why is this battle being lost? What can be more engaging than the nonstandard *Tell it like it is*? What can seem more pedantic than the standard *Tell it as it is*? Breathes there a fight broadcaster who would not say,

"Rocky looks *like* he'll never get off the deck"? A broadcaster who says, "Rocky looks *as if* he will not rise to his feet" will soon have to find another line of work.

So what is all the fuss about? Any grammarian will tell you that in these constructions *like* is properly a preposition and *as* a conjunction. You will find it easy to keep this distinction in mind if you recall that the grammatical construction following a preposition does not normally contain a verb—"*like* a dog," "*of* the people, *by* the people, and *for* the people." Not a verb in sight. When clauses are joined by a conjunction, however, you soon come upon a verb.

- The suit fits *like* a glove. (*Correct.* No verb after the preposition *like*.)
- He promised to return *as* he was leaving. (*Correct.* Verb *was leaving* after the conjunction *as*.)

To be sure, nobody makes the mistake of saying or writing, "The suit fits *as* a glove" or "He promised to return *like* he was leaving." The two sentences supplied above were intended to establish that, in the first example, *like* is a preposition and that, in the second example, *as* is a conjunction. In formal writing, *like* must not be used as a conjunction—especially where *as if* is needed.

Nonstandard The dean accepted full responsibility for the unfortunate incident, *like* any competent adminstrator would. (Preposition *like* must be replaced.)

Standard The dean accepted full responsibility for the unfortunate incident, *as* any competent adminstrator would. (Conjunction *as* in place of *like*.)

Nonstandard. They ate dish after dish of ice cream *like* it was going out of style. (Again, *like* must be replaced.)

Standard They ate dish after dish of ice cream *as if* it were going out of style. (Notice also that *were*, a subjunctive form, has replaced the past form *was*. Ice cream was not going out of style, so the statement is a condition contrary to fact.)

Nonstandard For at least a year before the fatal heart attack, Dorothy lived *like* there was no tomorrow.

Standard For at least a year before the fatal heart attack, Dorothy lived *as if* there were no tomorrow. (Again, the subjunctive *were* has replaced *was*. As far as we know, there will always be a tomorrow.)

The beginning writer who habitually uses *like* as a subordinating conjunction through ignorance rather than preference is best advised to treat *like* and *as* in the traditional manner. Let advertising writers and other linguistically influential people experiment all they want, but college teachers are not eager to give up the distinction between these two words.

LINKING VERB

A *linking*, or *copulative*, verb is one that indicates a relationship between a subject and the predicate adjective or predicate noun that complements, or completes, the verb. A linking verb performs no action. The most frequently used linking verb is *be*. Others include *feel, seem, prove, look, taste*, and *appear*.

- He *was* a retired lawyer. (The complement *lawyer* is a predicate noun.)
- She *seemed* well when we saw her last week. (The complement *well* is a predicate adjective.)
- The captain *proved* a valuable friend in later years. (The complement *friend* is a predicate noun.)
- Her desserts *taste* good, just as her mother's did. (The complement *good* is a predicate adjective. Be aware that *taste* and *feel* can also function as transitive verbs, verbs that take an object. See below.)
- The audience *appeared* restless during the first act. (The complement *restless* is a predicate adjective.)

Many linking verbs can also function as *transitive* or *intransitive* verbs. (See TRANSITIVE AND INTRANSITIVE VERBS.)

- He *felt* the wall gingerly. (The verb *felt* is transitive. Its object is *wall*. The verb *felt* is modified by the adverb *gingerly*.)
- Sally *proved* her solution by doing the problem over again in another way. (The verb *proved* is transitive. Its object is *solution*. The verb *proved* is modified by *by doing the problem over again in another way*.)
- Mickey *tasted* the soup and pronounced it the best his grandmother had ever prepared. (The object of the transitive verb *tasted* is *soup*.)
- The sommelier *chilled* the wine before serving it. (The verb *chilled* is transitive. Its object is *wine*. The verb *chilled* is modified by *before serving it*.)
- We *chilled* quickly in the brisk wind. (The verb *chilled* is intransitive. It is modified by *quickly*.)

- He *appeared* late in the day. (The verb *appeared* is intransitive. It is modified by *late in the day*.)
- They *looked* until they tired of the sight. (The verb *looked* is intransitive. It is modified by *until they tired of the sight*.)

LITERAL, FIGURATIVE

As sometimes happens in the development of a language, an English adjective and its adverbial form are on their way to acquiring a sense entirely opposite to their primary sense. The adjective *literal* and the adverb *literally* are being used as substitutes for *figurative* and *figuratively*.

In defining *literal*, even the most permissive lexicographers use such phrases as "restricted to the exact, stated meaning" and, they typically add, "not figurative." In defining *figurative*, they use such phrases as "based on, like, or containing a figure or figures of speech; metaphorical." Clearly, *literal* and *figurative* are represented as antonyms.

More and more, however, public officials, faceless radio voices, television newscasters, and people we consider our friends treat us to examples of what may be called verbal role reversal:

- The homeless man found himself *literally* sitting next to a pot of gold. It was $20,200 in cash. (*Literally a pot of gold*? Surely the pot of gold many people search for is a metaphor for wealth, that is, a *figurative pot of gold*.)
- When the Scud missiles began to fall, I was *literally* petrified. (*Literally petrified*? Literally "converted into a substance of stony character"? No one who is literally petrified can say these words or any others. Surely this use of *petrified* is metaphoric, that is, *figuratively petrified*.)

In your own speech, and particularly in your writing, you are advised to steer clear of this confusion.

LOAN, LEND

Loan in formal English is a noun, *lend* a verb. In general American speech, however, *loan* is regularly used as a verb.

General The banker *loaned* me the money. (verb)
Formal The banker *lent* me the money. (verb)
The banker decided to authorize the *loan*. (noun)

Editors and teachers prefer *lend* as a verb, *loan* as a noun.

LOWER CASE

Teachers and editors use the abbreviation *l.c.* or draw a slanted line through a capital letter to indicate that *lower case* (small letters) should be used in place of *upper case* (capital letters).

M

METAPHOR

A metaphor is a figure of speech in which a term or phrase is applied to someone or something to which it is not literally applicable. (See LITERAL, FIGURATIVE.)

- Norman was a *pussycat* at home, a *lion* in battle. (Norman literally was neither a pussycat nor a lion. The metaphor conveys the idea that Norman, a quiet man at home, showed great courage on the battlefield.)

Related to the metaphor is the simile, which is a figure of speech in which two unlike things are explicitly compared. The comparison is made explicit by use of *like* or *as*.

- Norman fought *like* a *lion*. (Norman, of course, did not use his claws and jaws. He did, however, show the courage and ferocity of a lion.)

A third figure of speech is hyperbole, which is gross exaggeration or overstatement that is not meant to be taken literally.

- *Mountains of unwashed dishes* awaited them at home, but they could not summon up the courage to face the job of washing them. (Fortunately, no matter how long we delay, unwashed dishes never reach high enough to literally be described as mountains.)

MIXED USAGE

Mixed usage is a term used to describe the error of mixing different levels of usage, for example, words or structures from informal writing that appear in formal writing, nonstandard words that appear in general writing. Once such errors are pointed out by a teacher or editor, the writer usually understands why the targeted locutions are inappropriate.

Yet we may ask, "How are we to know something is inappropriate while we are writing it?" A question of this sort is difficult to answer, but some help is possible if writers will read their first drafts aloud slowly and listen to every word. If anything suspicious is heard, then a good recent dictionary can be counted on to establish the level of usage for words that are other than standard. If such a dictionary does not provide a usage label for a word you look up, then the word may be considered standard. If it is not standard, such labels as *informal* or *slang* or *offensive* will be used in the entry. The prefatory material in your dictionary will identify and explain all the usage labels it provides.

If you cannot readily find a substitute in your own store of words, consult your thesaurus and, as always, read the dictionary definition of any substitute word you find before using the word in your paper. Wide reading and experience in writing will gradually improve any writer's diction and finally eliminate the mistake of mixed usage.

MODAL AUXILIARY

A modal auxiliary is a verb that performs a helping function when used with the base form of another verb. The combination of modal auxiliary and the base form expresses distinctions of MOOD.

- I *may leave* tomorrow.
- I *should leave* tomorrow.
- I *will leave* tomorrow. (The base form *leave* plus the modal auxiliaries *may*, *should*, and *will* provide different grammatical moods and, therefore, distinctly different meanings.

Modal auxiliaries always occur with other verbs—whether present or implied—and they have no compound forms.

- I *may*.
- I *should*.
- I *will*. (The base form *leave* is implied in all these examples.)

The most common modal auxiliaries are *can*, *could*, *may*, *might*, *must*, *ought*, *shall*, *should*, *will*, and *would*.

MODIFIERS

Modifiers are words or groups of words that limit, describe, or make more specific any of the main sentence elements. One problem with modifiers is that writers may fail to use the modifiers correctly. Another problem may result from failing to place modifiers close enough to the words they modify. The second problem is commonly called a *misplaced modifier*. The resulting confusion for the reader may be serious. Consider the following examples, in which the modifiers are italicized:

Incorrect The infield is designed *for right-handed fielders, with the exception of first base*. (An infield may be designed for right-handed fielders, but it cannot be designed for first base. It can be designed for first basemen.)

Correct The infield is designed *for right-handed fielders, with the exception of left-handed first basemen.* (Now we are designing fields for fielders, not for fielders and first base.)

Correct With the exception of first base, the infield is designed *for right-handed fielders.* (By moving one of the modifiers, first base is correctly understood to be part of the infield.)

Correct The infield, *with the exception of first base,* is designed *for right-handed fielders.* (Same comment.)

Incorrect Meeting the agent early, the dinner was over *in half an hour.* (The dinner appears to be meeting the agent.)

Correct Since we met the agent early, the dinner was over *in half an hour.* (Now we have met the agent early.)

It is worth pointing out that in all these sentences, as in most sentences you will ever write, the article *the* is used freely. When you consider that an article is a modifier and that you would confuse your readers hopelessly by moving *the* willy-nilly within a sentence, you must see that all modifiers must be treated with the same respect.

MOOD

Mood refers to the changes in the form of a verb to denote the attitude of the writer toward the statement being made. English employs the indicative, subjunctive, and imperative moods. The sentences that follow illustrate the uses of all three moods.

Indicative He *remained* silent. (statement)

Indicative Did he *remain* silent? (question)

Subjunctive If he *were* here, I am sure he would not remain silent on this question. (condition contrary to fact)

Subjunctive If only he *were* here, things would go better. (wish)

Subjunctive The meeting will go more smoothly, provided he *pay* close attention to the business at hand. (supposition)

Subjunctive Let peace *come* to all the world! (exhortation)

Imperative Leave this room at once! (command)

Imperative Please *stay* in your seats until the examination is over. (strong request)

MORPHEME

The smallest meaningful unit in a language is called a *morpheme.* It applies to words and to units that may combine with words. English morphemes include *-ing, -s, -ed, -ness, -ly, un-,* and *im-.*

MOST

Most is colloquial—therefore incorrect in formal writing—when used in the sense of *almost*, *nearly*, or *very*.

Incorrect He was *most* exhausted.
Correct He was *nearly* exhausted.
Correct He was *almost* exhausted.

Most has its proper usage as the superlative form of *more*, as in *He was most alert in the morning*. In the incorrect example above, *He was most exhausted*, there is no question of degrees of exhaustion. *Exhausted* describes a state much like that described by *dead*—people can be *nearly* dead or *almost* dead, but not *very* dead or *most* dead. Once people reach the point of exhaustion, they cannot go beyond that point. Of course, they may think they are exhausted and yet be able to go on. Anyone who has watched an apparently exhausted marathon runner catch sight of the finish line will undertsand this phenomenon.

MS, MS.

The abbreviation for manuscript is MS. The abbreviation for manuscripts is MSS. Both abbreviations carry a period.

Ms. is not an abbreviation. It is a title of respect for a woman. Ms., unlike Miss or Mrs. does not indicate marital status. The plural of Ms. is Mses.

MYSELF

Myself is one of a group of reflexive pronouns (see PRONOUN), which intensify the pronoun or noun to which they refer. Reflexive pronouns are not restricted to the first person singular.

- I *myself* will do all the work.
- I will do all the work *myself*.
- You *yourself* will do all the work.
- You will do all the work *yourself*.
- Sally *herself* will do all the work.
- Joe is going to do all the work *himself*.
- We will do all the work *ourselves*.
- They will do all the work *themselves*.

N

NECESSARY

The word *necessary* is frequently misspelled. One *c* and two *s*'s.

NICE

In general and informal writing, the word *nice* has lost its meaning and should be avoided. Substitute more precise words.

> *Avoid* He is a *nice* fellow. (Just what do we intend here beyond conveying a general feeling that the fellow is not evil?)
>
> *Improved* He is a pleasant companion and generous to strangers. (Specific information is far better than vague modifiers.)
>
> *Avoid* What I want now is a *nice* cup of tea. (Perhaps the best solution here is to eliminate rather than replace *nice*. Was there ever a cup of tea that could be improved by adding a meaningless modifier?)
>
> *Improved* What I want now is a cup of *strong* tea *that has been properly brewed*. (By using two meaningful modifiers, we are specifying the kind of tea desired.)

NO-COMPOUNDS

Nobody, nothing, none, and *nowhere* are written as one word. *Nobody* and *nothing* are pronouns that are treated as singulars.

- Nobody *understands* the lesson. (Singular subject *nobody*, singular verb *understands*.)
- Nothing *is* too good for their children. (Singular subject *nothing*, singular verb *is*.)

None, also a pronoun, has long been treated both as singular and plural. In educated speech and writing, only when *none* is intended to mean "not any" or "not one" is it treated as singular.

> *Correct* Of all the writers whose work I admire, *none* has received adequate critical recognition. (The pronoun *none* here means "not one writer" and so is treated as singular.)

When *none* is intended to mean "not any things" or "not any persons"—notice the plural "things" and "persons"—*none* is most often treated as plural. Purists will insist that *none* always be treated as singular, but their preference is usually perceived as pedantry.

Correct None of the writers whose work I admire *have* received critical recognition. (The pronoun *none* here means "not any writers" and so is treated as plural).

Stiffly Correct All suggestions as to where the child may have been during the incident are being investigated scrupulously, but thus far *none has been found* helpful. (The pronoun *none* here means "not one suggestion," so it is treated as singular: *none has been found helpful*. Most people, including the writers of this book, would be uncomfortable with this construction.)

Nowhere is usually an adverb, so it is free of pronoun problems.

- *Nowhere* was the child to be found. (The adverb *nowhere* modifies the infinitive *to be found*.)

Nowhere is also used as a noun.

- The filly came from *nowhere* to win the Kentucky Derby. (The noun *nowhere* functions as object of the preposition *from*.)

NOHOW

Nohow is an example of nonstandard English, which is language unacceptable in general and formal speech and writing. It is acceptable to use *nohow* or any other nonstandard expression in writing when the writer is being jocular or when the writer is reporting speech by a person who uses nonstandard expressions.

- "He couldn't do the problem *nohow*." (Not only is *nohow* nonstandard English, but the sentence provides an example of a *double negative*. You would not write, "He could *not* do the problem *no* way he tried"—a double negative—but you might write, "He could *not* do the problem *any* way he tried."

NONSTANDARD ENGLISH

Nonstandard English is language unacceptable in general and formal writing. Except for quotation from nonstandard sources, use standard English in your formal writing. Jocularity that depends on use of nonstandard English (see NOHOW) is not customary in general or formal writing.

NOUN

The noun is the part of speech that names a person, place, thing, or abstraction. It generally forms its plural in *s* and its possessive with an apostrophe: *trees*, *Frank's friend*. Nouns function as subject, object, object of a preposition, appositive (see APPOSITION), subjective complement, modifier, indirect object, or possessive.

NOUN CLAUSE

A noun clause is a clause that functions as a noun. In many instances noun clauses function as direct objects of such verbs as *believe, think, hope,* and *dream.* Other noun clauses function as subjects or as objects of a preposition. Most noun clauses are introduced by *that,* others by *who, whether,* and other conjunctions and pronouns. In the following sentences, noun clauses are italicized.

- She hoped *that they would arrive on time.* (The noun clause functions as direct object of the verb *hoped.*)
- *That Jose learned to swim in three weeks* pleased the coach. (The noun clause functions as subject of the verb *pleased.*)
- *Who would finally be chosen* remained a mystery until President Nixon made the announcement. (The noun clause functions as subject of the verb *remained.*)
- He was certain of *what he had heard.* (The noun clause functions as object of the preposition *of.*)

NOWHERE NEAR

The expression *nowhere near* is considered informal. In general and formal English, it is avoided.

Informal We got *nowhere near* the top.
General We did not get *near* the top.

NUMBER

Number is the grammatical concept of singular and plural for nouns, pronouns, possesive adjectives, and verbs. Number, an essential consideration in reference and agreement, is important in achieving clarity in your writing.

- *One* of the *boys who were approaching* graduation *has found* Latin grammar an insurmountable obstacle. (The verb *has found* agrees in number with *one,* its subject. The verb *were approaching* agrees in number with the pronoun *who,* its subject. We know that *who* is plural, because its antecedent is *boys,* a plural.)

Number as a Collective Noun

Notice that the noun *number* as a collective is taken as a singular or as a plural depending on the intention of the writer.

- A *number* of foreign writers *were denied* access to a meeting held in the United States. (Here, *number* is intended as a "certain number of people.")
- The *number* of her accomplishments *is* astonishing in one so young. (Here, *number* is taken as a unit.).

O

OBJECT

Nouns and pronouns function as objects of verbs, prepositions, verbals, and certain adjectives.)

Object of a Verb

The alumnae donated a *building* to the university. (The noun *building* functions as object of the verb *donated*.)

They found the *solution* difficult. (The noun *solution* functions as object of the verb *found*.)

She wished *that they would leave* so she could get on with her research. (The noun clause *that they would leave* functions as object of the verb *wished*.)

Susan finds *you* objectionable. (The pronoun *you* functions as object of the verb *finds*.)

Object of a Preposition

The couple went to the *movies*. (The noun *movies* functions as object of the preposition *to*.)

His eyeglasses were found on the *shelf*. (The noun *shelf* functions as object of the preposition *on*.)

From *what they could gather*, no prize would be awarded that year. (The noun clause *what they could gather* functions as object of the preposition *from*.)

For *her*, salary was a secondary consideration. (The pronoun *her* functions as object of the preposition *for*.)

Object of a Verbal

Sam loved to run the *mile*. (The noun *mile* functions as object of the infinitive *to run*.)

Rebecca liked swimming the *river* before breakfast. (The noun *river* functions as object of the gerund *swimming*.)

Participles, the third type of verbal, are used as adjectives and do not function as objects.

Object of Adjective

Gloria found the automobile not worth the *price*. (The noun *price* functions as object of the adjective *worth*.)

ONE

The pronoun *one* can be used personally (*one* finds all lies objectionable) or impersonally (*one* is enough). *One* can cause trouble in two ways: awkward repetition and faulty number of the verb of which *one* is the subject.

> *Awkward One* can only ask for things *one* wants badly if *one* is willing to risk losing it completely.
>
> *Improved* Anyone who wants something badly should risk asking for it.

The awkward example concocted above is not intended to suggest that you may never use *one* in a personal sense. In fact, *one* is often used in that sense, but notice the way awkward repetition of *one* is avoided by combining *one* with other pronouns in the following realistic examples:

- *One* has to get *his* (or *her*) own way once in a while. (The practice of shifting away from *one* to another pronoun with the same referent is well established. It was long the practice to use *his* in sentences such as this when the sex of the referent was unclear.)
- *One* has to be true to *himself* if *he* is to look at *himself* in the shaving mirror each morning. (The practice of the previous example is expanded to show that the pronouns used in place of *one* or *oneself* should be used consistently. The language of the example—*shaving mirror*—also appears to make it clear that the person spoken of is male.)
- Without any knowledge of what is going on, *one* often finds *her* progress impeded by sexist attitudes in high places. (The referent of *one* must be taken as female in this context.)

One is often used with a plural in a modifying prepositional phrase, as in *one of those who*. The referent of *who* is the plural *those* in this construction, not the singular *one*, but many writers and speakers tend to ignore this grammatical analysis. Whether the change in practice is due to sloppiness or to a deliberate effort is not known, but the *New York Times* and other publications of high standing appear to be ignoring the old conventions of agreement and reference.

> *Formal English* Sherman was *one* of those *who* made clear *their stands* on the nomination. (The antecedent of *who* is the plural pronoun *those*, so *their stands* is expected.)
>
> *General English* Sherman was *one* of those *who* made clear *his*

stand on the nomination. (What is the antecedent of *who*? The answer is still *those*. Notwithstanding, general writing ignores this fact, which calls for the plural *their stands* rather than the singular *his stand*.)

You can be certain your teachers and most editors will prefer the formal practice in regard to *one of those who* and similar constructions.

ONLY

In formal English, *only* is placed directly next to the construction modified.

- She has *only* three weeks left before she reports for induction. (To say *she only has* would imply that she has nothing else but three weeks. She surely has something besides time—health, clothing, and many other things.)
- *Only* one electric light bulb was left intact after the vandals finished their work. (Just think of the change in meaning if the sentence read: *One electric light bulb was left intact only after the vandals finished their work* or *One electric light bulb was left intact after the vandals finished their only work*.)

In some cases, of course, the position of the word *only* can change in a limited way without destroying the intended meaning.

- Such words are used *only* in formal English.
- Such words are *only* used in formal English.
- Such words are used in formal English *only*.

While English generally is a demanding language, we are not hamstrung by its requirements. The important question to answer in regard to style is: Where must I place modifiers to achieve precisely the effect I want to achieve?

OR

Or is a coordinating conjunction used to connect two independent clauses or to connect two grammatically similar elements. Consider the uses of *or* as a conjunction and as a connective.

Conjunction
Humanity will find a way to settle disputes peacefully, *or* wars will continue to be fought periodically with great loss of lives. (*Or* connects two independent clauses.)
We can all go in one car, *or* you can take your car and I will take mine. (*Or* connects two independent clauses, *We can all go in*

OR

> *one car* and *you can take your car. And*—also a coordinating conjunction—connects the second independent clause and the third, *I will take mine.*)

Connective

Either Jonathan or Daniel will call for you. (Or connects two proper nouns, Jonathan and Daniel, used as subjects of will call.)

We can take the luggage with us or send it on ahead. (Or connects two elements of a compound verb, take and send.)

They could not decide whether to donate their money or their paintings to the charity. (Or connects two nouns, money and paintings, used as objects of the infinitive donate.)

Number of Connected Elements

When *or* connects two elements used together as subject of a verb, the verb agrees with the number of the element closer to it.

- Two short novels *or* a single full-length novel *is* necessary to fulfill course requirements. (Plural noun *novels* and singular noun *novel* are connected by *or*. Since *novel* is closer to the verb, a singular verb is used: *a single full-length novel is necessary*.)
- One long novel *or* two short ones *are* required. (The plural *two short ones* is closer to the verb: *two short ones are required*.)

Either ... or

Or is frequently used in combination with *either*.

- *Either* you stay *or* I will. (One or the other person will stay.)
- *Either* both cars are repaired *or* none is. (Both are repaired, or neither is.)

And/Or

Or is so frequently combined with *and* in legal, business, and technical writing that the word *and/or* is increasingly seen, conveying the sense of *one or the other* or *both*. Formal writing outside these specialized types of writing does not usually accept this locution.

Avoid Failure of the odometer *and/or* the speedometer is not considered serious under most conditions. (The sentence suggests that failure of one or both of the instruments will not prove hazardous.)

Avoid The plaintiff *and/or* the defendant will appear in court tomorrow. (In this sentence, as in almost all other *and/or* constructions, the writer could have made the meaning clear by using *and* alone.)

Avoid Homes *and/or* structures designed for agricultural uses are prohibited under the new ordinance. (In this sentence, the writer could have made the meaning clear by using *and* alone.)

Most editors and teachers frown on *and/or* constructions. To avoid *and/or* in formal writing, the first two examples could have been expressed as follows:

Better Failure of the speedometer, the odometer, or both will not usually endanger a driver.

Better The plaintiff, defendant, or both must appear in court tomorrow.

ORGANIZATION

After *clarity*, the mark *org*, meaning *poor organization*, is the English teacher's harshest critical label. A well organized paper reflects careful thinking, planning, and execution. Writers whose work is marked *org* would do well to prepare an outline before beginning to write, follow the outline while writing, and read the first draft of every paper carefully, taking pains to determine whether it is logically and convincingly organized. When the final draft is ready, the writer should read once more to determine whether the paper still makes a tight, coherent statement.

OUT-OF CONSTRUCTIONS

Constructions employing *out of* are hyphenated only when they are used as modifiers preceding the element modified.

- That book is *out of date*. (This construction must not be hyphenated. It follows the verb *is* and does not function as a modifier. The phrase functions as a complement—specifically, a predicate adjective.)
- Some people thought that the Lawrenceville stories were *out-of-date* accounts of a dead age. (*Out-of-date* modifies *accounts*, which it precedes.)

The following examples contrast the use of modifiers before and after the element modified to emphasize that *out-of* constructions are hyphenated only when they precede the element modified, not when they follow it.

111

- An *out-of-date* design such as the one you are suggesting will not attract many sophisticated clients. (The modifier *out-of-date* precedes *design*, the noun it modifies.)
- Few sophisticated clients will be attracted to designs *as out of date as the one you have suggested*. (The modifier *as out of date as the one you have suggested*, a subordinate clause, follows *designs*, the noun it modifies.)

P

PARAGRAPH

Teachers use the word *paragraph*, the abbreviation *par.*, or the symbol ¶ to indicate a mistake in paragraphing. A common mistake in writing is that of arbitrarily breaking off a discussion before development of an idea is complete. Another mistake is that of using the final sentence of a paragraph to introduce an idea that is developed in the following paragraph. Good writers know that effective transition between ideas is essential for achieving COHERENCE, but transitional elements should be supplied at the beginning of a section or paragraph, not at the end of the previous unit.

How, then, does a writer decide when to begin and when to end a paragraph? A good paragraph provides full development of one idea or of one major portion of an idea worthy of presentation in its own paragraph, a stylistic unit that usually comprises several sentences.

There is, however, no single prescribed length for a paragraph. Ideas differ in importance and complexity, and the best length for a given paragraph reflects the importance and complexity of the idea to be expressed. If an idea requires few sentences to present completely, then a paragraph containing just a few sentences will do. (If you adopt this criterion and find that your paragraphs habitually are quite short, you should examine the ideas you are presenting to see whether some of them can be combined to make fewer, somewhat longer paragraphs.)

By contrast, when an idea is complex, a long paragraph may be called for to express the idea adequately. Even so, most modern writers avoid the interminable paragraphs that were fashionable in the nineteenth century. They recognize that the attention span of the reader is finite, so they break their development of a complex idea into several paragraphs but make certain that the paragraphs are coherently linked. As a further help for the reader, writers will intentionally include relatively short, understandable sentences within the paragraphs.

A word of caution: Increasingly there is a tendency to make paragraphs exceedingly short—a pair of sentences, even a single sentence. This practice may be all right for newspaper readers, but it is difficult to believe that the clarity of formal papers can be improved by consistently organizing paragraphs in this manner. Readers faced with extremely short paragraphs—and sentences—may feel more like tennis referees than members of an interested audience in search of mature ideas. Yet, when the development of an idea calls for it, a single paragraph comprising a single short sentence can achieve desirable emphasis. Needless to say, few situations call for using this stylistic device, so you must think hard before you employ it.

If the discussion of paragraph length has not given you a definitive guideline to follow, be advised that in this matter you must be your own final arbiter. When reading a first draft of a paper, ask yourself (1) do your paragraphs say what you want them to say and (2) do they pass the Goldilocks Test—not too short, not too long, but just right.

PARALLEL CONSTRUCTION

Elements performing similar grammatical functions should have similar grammatical forms.

Faulty Parallelism The educational system often overtaxes teachers with large classes, outdated textbooks, and with doing excessive clerical work. (This sentence contains a series, the first two elements of which are cast in noun form, *large classes* and *outdated textbooks*. The third element of the series is cast in the form of a gerund phrase, *doing excessive clerical work*.)

Correct Parallelism The educational system often overtaxes teachers with large classes, outdated textbooks, and excessive clerical work. (Now the series offers three noun phrases: *large classes*, *outdated textbooks*, and *excessive clerical work*.)

Faulty Parallelism The architect proposed a school functional in design, attractive to students, and which is superior in regard to location compared with other schools in the district. (The series contains three modifiers. Two of them are phrases, *functional in design* and *attractive to students*, and the third is a clause, *which is superior in regard to location compared with other schools in the district*.)

Correct Parallelism The architect proposed a school superior in design, attractiveness, and location compared with other district schools. (Now the series comprises three prepositional phrases, consisting of three nouns—*design*, *attractiveness*, *location*—that all serve as objects of a single preposition, *in*.)

Faulty Parallelism Most of the students and the girls in the school were enthusiastic about the project. (The words *students* and *girls* are both nouns, but girls surely are students.)

Correct Parallelism Most of the male and female students were enthusiastic about the project. (Now *students* is modified by a pair of adjectives, *male* and *female*.)

PARAPHRASE

A paraphrase is a restatement in one's own words of something said or written by another person. Paraphrase differs from direct quotation in two ways: in paraphrasing, the words must be one's own, and the paraphrase should be shorter and—for the context in which it will appear—better than the original. Of course, the paraphrase must be faithful to the meaning of the original. If a paraphrase is used for a class paper or for publication, the original material should be identified and cited in a footnote.

PARENTHESES

Parentheses are used to separate material from a sentence when the material is too far removed from the subject under discussion to be enclosed in commas or dashes. Additions, explanations, and informative asides are punctuated by parentheses. Some forms of citations and footnotes as well as enumerations also employ parentheses.

Addition

Or what is there apart from the traditions of dungeoned warriors and kings (which will not wholly account for it) that makes the White Tower of London tell so much more strongly on the imagination of a traveled American...?

—Melville, *Moby-Dick*

Explanatory Information

The young soldier returned to Rivière du Loup (Wolf River), where he had a small homestead.

Informative Aside

Insofar as Kipling grasps this, he simply sets it down to "the intense selfishness of the lower classes" (his own phrase).

—Orwell, "Rudyard Kipling"

Citations and Footnotes

Parentheses are used to enclose citations included in the text of a research paper.

Lady Gregory said that if the reception of the play improved, it would come off on Saturday, but if it did not, it would be played until it received a fair hearing (*Irish Independent,* Feb. 1, 1907).

Parentheses enclose the place and date of publication in footnotes.

Jack Kerouac, *Doctor Sax* (New York, 1959), p. 54.

Enumerations

Parentheses are sometimes used to enclose numbers or letters in an enumeration within a text: (1), (2); (a), (b).

PARTICIPLES

A participle is a verbal adjective with forms that can show both past and present tense, as well as active and passive voice.

	Active	*Passive*
Present	cleaning	being cleaned
Past	cleaned	having been cleaned

Participles may either be used as modifiers or in combination with verbs. When participles are combined with auxiliary verbs—*I am cleaning, she has cleaned,* etc.—they indicate tense but they do not function as adjectives.

Modifiers

The forms and voices of the participle are used as modifiers in a variety of constructions.

- *Encouraged* by their initial success, the authors started another book. (*Encouraged* modifies *authors.*)
- *Having been rebuffed,* the candidate decided to return to Massachusetts. (*Having been rebuffed* modifies *candidate.*)
- The *insulting* performance was too much for most of us to take. (*Insulting* modifies *performance.*)
- The *smiling* candidate answered the loaded question, unaware that he was about to doom his candidacy. (*Smiling* modifies *candidate.*)

Introductory Participles

Introductory participles refer to the grammatical subject of the sentence.

Incorrect Closing the paragraph, the force of lightning was compared with the force of water. (The grammatical subject of the sentence is *force*, and the verb is *was compared*. It appears that the participle *closing* refers to *force* of lightning. The sentence makes no sense.)

Correct Closing the paragraph, the author compared the force of lightning with the force of water. (Now the grammatical subject is *author*, and authors can close paragraphs. Thus, the participle *closing* correctly refers to the grammatical subject of the sentence, *author*.)

Incorrect Looking at the sun through the window of a heated room, the outside temperature may appear high when it is not. (The participle *looking* seems to refer to *temperature*, which is the grammatical subject of the sentence. But *temperatures* are not capable of *looking*.)

Correct Looking at the sun through the window of a heated room, you may think the temperature is high outside when it is not. (Now *looking* refers to *you*, a grammatical subject capable of *looking*.)

Absolute Construction

Absolute constructions—usually consisting of a noun modified by a participle—have only a general relationship to the rest of the words of the sentence.

- *The principal checkpoints having been passed*, the group dispersed without further interference. (The absolute construction does not modify the independent clause or any element of that clause.)

This type of construction is practically a direct translation from the Latin *ablative absolute*, frequently encountered in Caesar's writings. As a result it tends to appear excessively formal or literary. Most often we change a construction such as the one above and place the sense of an absolute construction in a subordinate clause:

- *When the principal checkpoints had been passed*, the group dispersed without further interference. (The subordinate clause modifies *dispersed*.)

Loosely related introductory participial phrases are also classified as absolutes.

- *Judging by his face*, the young actor must have been no more than twenty years old.

- *Taking all the circumstances into account*, her angry response can be considered defensible.

Participle as Element of Verb Form

The *present participle* is used with the verb *be* to form progressive tenses. Three of the *active progressive tenses* are illustrated here.

- He *is beckoning* to you from across the street. (present progressive)
- A national flag *has been flying* above the consulate since the troops entered the city. (present perfect progressive)
- The fastest ship in the race *was nearing* the finish line when a gust of wind turned her abeam. (past progressive)

The *past participle* is used with the verb *be* to form the passive voice. Three tenses in the *passive voice* are illustrated here.

- The popular incumbent *is favored* to win reelection by a record majority. (present passive)
- Montreal long *has been favored* by United States tourists in Canada. (present perfect passive)
- Unfortunately, the guest speaker, a handicapped woman, *was delayed* at the airport. (past passive)

PASSIVE VERBS

Passive verbs are formed by the *past participle* and the appropriate form of the verb *be*. Passive verbs do not transfer action from the subject to some other sentence element. They indicate the manner in which the subject is itself acted upon.

In grammatical terms, if we think of the element receiving the action of a verb as the *logical object*, then the subject of a passive verb is a *logical object* occupying the *grammatical subject* position. In turn, the *logical subject* in a passive construction occupies a position as *object of a preposition* following the verb, or it does not appear at all. Examine the following sentence:

- The ball *was struck* by the little girl.

Who performed the action? The *girl*. What about the *ball*? The *ball* was struck. So the *ball*, which is the logical object, is in the subject position. The verb is therefore passive.

In the active voice, the sentence would read:

- The little girl *struck* the ball.

The passive voice, then, shifts the emphasis from the logical subject to the logical object. This shift of emphasis is sometimes of great use in writing—particularly when we are writing of *things that are happening to someone or something*, rather than writing about *who is doing something to someone or something*. Much of the writing in science falls logically into this category, since scientists are not ordinarily concerned with *who or what has done something* but with *what has been done*.

On the other hand, thoughtless use of the passive often results in awkward, unemphatic sentences. In the following example, taken from a work in the social sciences, the passive voice is used in the first sentence to focus the reader's attention on the logical subject, which is the subject of the passive verb. In the second sentence, the emphasis shifts away from that logical subject in a manner that makes the reader wonder why this was done.

> By 1887 Durkheim *was recognized* in the field as an outstanding sociologist, and he began his thirty-year university career. At the University of Bordeaux, a course in the social sciences *was created* for him. Adapted from Kardiner & Preble, *They Studied Man* (New York, 1951), p. 110.

In the first sentence the subject of the passive verb—also the logical subject of that verb—is *Durkheim*, focusing attention on him. In the second sentence, the subject of the passive verb *was created* is the logical object, *course*—the course did not do the creating; the course was created. The logical subject of *was created*—the person or organization that did the creating—does not appear in this passive construction. So a *course was created*, but by whom we do not know. In addition, attention has been shifted away from *Durkheim* in the first sentence to *course* in the second sentence.

Would readers not have benefited from recasting the second sentence in the active voice so that their attention would still be directed at *Durkheim*, the logical subject of the pair of sentences? If that is done, the two sentences become:

> By 1887 Durkheim *was recognized* in the field as an outstanding sociologist, and he began his thirty-year university career. At the University of Bordeaux, Durkheim *initiated* a course in the social sciences that *had been created* especially for him.

Notice that there is no stylistic rule against mixing active and passive verbs. The original selection already had the active verb *began* in the second independent clause of the first sentence. In the rewritten sentences, this active verb is retained, the independent clause of the second sentence is given an active verb, and the new subordinate clause is given the passive verb *had been created*. Through these changes we have achieved our stylistic purpose: to concentrate attention throughout on the logical subject, *Durkheim*.

Use the passive voice *only* when you wish to emphasize the person or object affected by the action of a verb. Consider the passive verb in the next example and the active verb in the example that follows it.

- Three hundred civilians *were killed*. (Passive voice. It is the fate of the civilians we are interested in, not the means by which they were killed.)
- Bombs *killed* three hundred civilians. (Active voice. Now we have found out what caused the deaths.)

Make your choice between active and passive when you have determined which element you wish to emphasize in a sentence.

PERSON

Pronouns are classified by *person* and *number*. *Person* identifies who is indicated by the pronoun. *Number* indicates whether the pronoun is singular or plural. Personal pronouns are the only ones that have elaborate inflectional systems; other pronouns change forms only for the objective and possessive cases.

First Person

Case	*Singular*	*Plural*
Subjective	I	we
Possessive	mine	ours
Objective	me	us

Second Person

Case	*Singular*	*Plural*
Subjective	you	you
Possessive	yours	yours
Objective	you	you

Third Person

Case	*Masculine*	*Feminine*	*Neuter*	*Plural*
Subjective	he	she	it	they
Possessive	his	hers	its	theirs
Objective	him	her	it	them

Verbs indicate person and number only for the third person singular of the present tense:

- I wash
- you wash
- he, she, or it washes

Nouns are third person and regularly inflect to indicate singular or plural.

PERSONIFICATION

Personification is the stylistic device of attributing human characteristics to abstract ideas, objects, or animals. Used more in poetry than in prose, personification is a worthwhile technique in the hands of a professional, but it is may appear awkward when undertaken by a beginning writer, who resorts to clichés when attempting to use personification. Thus, for such a writer, *time* is always *flying*, *tyranny* is always *crying out for vengeance*, *pines* always *whisper* and *stand alone against the sky*, and *an oppressed land* is always *bleeding*.

See what a poet does with personification:

> When Time began to rant and rage,
> The measure of her flying feet
> Made Ireland's heart begin to beat;
> And Time bade all his candles flare
> To light a measure here and there;
> —Yeats, "To Ireland in the Coming Times"

While a writer of prose rarely sustains personification to this extent, extended personification in prose is known. Here is a portion of a speech by Mark Twain dealing with New England weather:

> There is a sumptuous variety about the New England weather that compels the stranger's admiration—and regret. The weather is always doing something there; always attending strictly to business; always getting up new designs and trying them on people to see how they will go. But it gets through more business in Spring than in any other season. In the spring I have counted one hundred and thirty-six different kinds of weather inside of twenty-four hours.

PHENOMENON, PHENOMENA

Phenomenon is singular, *phenomena* plural. As time goes by, the plural form is used as a singular more and more frequently. The climax in this development will come when we hear a politician or radio commentator speak wisely about *phenomenas*. By then, the form *phenomenon* will be a verbal fossil.

Phenomenon originally meant "any object directly discernible through sight, smell, taste, etc.," but that meaning is rapidly losing ground to the sense of "an uncommon or abnormal person, thing, or occurrence—an inexplicable fact." The adjective *phenomenal* is usually intended in this sense.

PHRASAL VERB

A phrasal verb is any verb formed by an auxiliary plus an infinitive or past participle: *shall run, is pleased, has been searched*. Phrasal verbs are also called *periphrastic verbs*.

PHRASE

A phrase, a group of words without a subject or predicate, may function as subject or object in a sentence or as modifier of another sentence element. There are four types of phrases: prepositional, participial, infinitive, and gerund.

Prepositional and participial phrases always function as modifiers. Infinitive phrases may function as modifiers or as subjects or objects. Gerund phrases always function as subjects or objects.

Prepositional Phrase

A prepositional phrase is composed of a preposition, its object, and the modifiers of the object.

- He came *out of the house*, went *to the shore*, and bought a box *of cookies*. (The first two prepositional phrases function as adverbs, modifying *came* and *went* respectively. The third functions as an adjective, modifying *box*.)

Participial Phrase

A participial phrase is composed of a present or past participle plus the object of the participle—if there is one—and any modifiers belonging to the unit.

- *Running to the window*, the children saw the car leave the road and jump the curb. (The participial phrase functions as modifier of *children*. The present participle *running* has no object, but is modified by the prepositional phrase *to the window*.)
- *Defeated in its third consecutive election*, the Independent Party decided to disband. (The participial phrase functions as modifier

of *Independent Party*. The past participle *defeated* has no object, but is modified by the prepositional phrase *in its third consecutive election*.)

A participial phrase can easily become a *dangling modifier*, often called a dangling participle, if the writer does not take care to attach the phrase to a recognizable sentence element.

> *Faulty* *Running to the window*, the car was seen leaving the road and jumping the curb. (The writer of this sentence would have us believe that the car ran to the window before leaving the road and jumping the curb.)

> *Faulty* *Defeated in the popular vote*, the election was thrown into the House of Representatives. (The election was not defeated in the popular vote. A candidate must have been defeated in the popular vote.)

Infinitive Phrase

An infinitive phrase is composed of an infinitive, the object of the infinitive—if an object is supplied—and any modifiers the phrase may include.

- *To return to his own room* seemed the only way for the freshman *to mollify the Dean of Residence Halls*. (The first infinitive phrase, *to return to his own room*, functions as the subject of the verb *seemed*. The infinitive *to return* is modified by a prepositional phrase, *to his own room*. The second infinitive phrase, *to mollify the Dean of Residence Halls*, modifies *way*. The noun *freshman* is the object of the preposition *for*, and the prepositional phrase *for the freshman* modifies the infinitive *mollify*.)
- Mary Kay decided *to order the chain saw* and *forget the cost*. (Infinitives *to order* and *forget*, objects *chain saw* and *cost*, modifiers *the* and *the*.)

Gerund Phrase

A gerund phrase is composed of a gerund, its object—if there is one—plus any modifiers.

- *His winning the game* caused joy in Mudville. (The gerund *winning* is the subject of the verb *caused*. The object of the gerund is *game*, which is modified by *the*.)

The gerund phrase in the preceding sentence functions as subject of *caused*. Notice the possessive adjective *his* before the gerund. In nonstandard English we may hear *Him winning the game caused joy in Mudville*. Such a construction cannot be used in a college paper unless it is part of a quotation.

PLAGIARISM

Plagiarism is the unauthorized use of a person's words or ideas and representing them as one's own. Avoid any suggestion of plagiarism by citing sources for the words or concepts you present if they are not entirely your own. (See PARAPHRASE.)

PLENTY

Plenty still survives in general and formal English as a noun: *America is a land of plenty*. As a modifier *plenty* is colloquial and should be avoided. A sentence such as *This is plenty good enough* is not permissible in general and formal writing.

PLURAL FORMS OF NOUNS

Nouns in English—with certain exceptions—form their plurals by adding *s* to the singular: *car, cars; horse, horses; alley, alleys*.

Exceptions and Problems

1. Nouns that end in a sounded *s* or in a sound close to the sound of *s* form their plurals by adding an extra, pronounced syllable so that the original ending can be heard. This practice includes nouns that end in *ch, dge, sh, ss, tch*, and *z* sounds.

- church, churches; torch, torches; porch, porches
- hedge, hedges; sludge, sludges
- lash, lashes; sash, sashes
- mass, masses; cutlass, cutlasses
- latch, latches; watch, watches
- adze, adzes; fuzz, fuzzes

2. For nouns ending in *y* preceded by a consonant, the *y* is changed to *i*, and *es* is added.

- ally, allies; sky, skies; fry, fries; body, bodies; belfry, belfries; county, counties

Note that nouns ending in *y* preceded by a vowel form their plurals in the conventional way.

- alloy, alloys; bay, bays.

3. Certain nouns ending in *o* preceded by a consonant form the plural by adding *es*.

- tomato, tomatoes; echo, echoes; mosquito, mosquitoes

Other nouns ending in *o* preceded by a consonant form the plural by adding *s*.

- canto, cantos; solo, solos; tremolo, tremolos

Certain nouns ending in *o* preceded by a consonant have both plural forms.

- zero, zeroes, zeros; cargo, cargoes, cargos; hobo, hoboes, hobos

Since there are several ways to form the plural of nouns ending in *o* preceded by a consonant, wise writers look to a dictionary for guidance to resolve any uncertainty.

4. Some nouns ending in *f* or *fe* change the *f* to *v* and add *s* or *es*.

- calf, calves; dwarf, dwarves; elf, elves; half, halves; leaf, leaves; loaf, loaves; scarf, scarves (also scarfs); self, selves; sheaf, sheaves; knife, knives; life, lives

Other nouns ending in *f* or *fe* have regular plurals.

- belief, beliefs; chief, chiefs; puff, puffs; roof, roofs; carafe, carafes; fife, fifes; safe, safes

5. Certain nouns—primarily survivors from Anglo-Saxon, which was more fully inflected than English—form the plural by adding an *n* sound, or by changing a vowel, or by changing a vowel and the final consonant.

- child, children; ox, oxen; foot, feet; man, men; woman, women; yeoman, yeomen; louse, lice; mouse, mice

6. Some nouns have the same form in the singular and plural.

- deer, fish (fishes *when referring to two or more species or kinds*), moose, quail, sheep, vermin

Other nouns have only one form, plural in appearance but treated as singular.

- series, species, trousers, scissors, news

7. Many words of foreign origin retain the plural form of the language from which they were borrowed. A few examples of borrowed words with foreign plural endings are:

addendum, addenda   antithesis, antitheses
automaton, automata   axis, axes
basis, bases   crisis, crises
criterion, criteria   ellipsis, ellipses
erratum, errata   exemplum, exempla
graffito, graffiti   hypothesis, hypotheses
kibbutz, kibbutzim   metamorphosis, metamorphoses
minutia, minutiae   ovum, ova
phenomenon, phenomena   putto, putti
radius, radii   synthesis, syntheses

To this list must be added two troublemakers:

- alumnus (male singular), alumna (female singular) alumni (male plural), alumnae (female plural)

As time goes by, some words of foreign origin begin to appear with both foreign and English plural forms. Some examples follow, with the more frequently encountered plural form given before the less frequent form.

- auditorium, auditoriums, auditoria
- bambino, bambinos, bambini
- corona, coronas, coronae
- crux, cruxes, cruces
- datum, data, datums
- focus, focuses, foci
- genus, genera, genuses
- gymnasium, gymnasiums, gymnasia
- helix, helixes, helices
- memorandum, memorandums, memoranda
- seraph, seraphs, seraphim
- supernova, supernovas, supernovae
- tableau, tableaux, tableaus
- thesaurus, thesauruses, thesauri

8. The plural forms of certain hyphenated terms trouble some writers. A few examples follow:

- counselor-at-law, counselors-at-law
- daughter-in-law, daughters-in-law
- father-in-law, fathers-in-law
- lady-in-waiting, ladies-in-waiting

- mother-in-law, mothers-in-law
- secretary-general, secretaries-general
- son-in-law, sons-in-law

PREDICATE

The predicate of a sentence or clause is made up of the verb, its modifiers, plus its direct and indirect objects or complement. Together these elements make a statement with respect to the subject. In the following examples, the predicates are shown in italics.

- Everything *comes to those who wait.*
- Good students *usually work hard in their courses.*
- The grieving parents *now appear better adjusted to their loss.*
- Physicians intent on treating their patients competently *will no longer work in that third-rate hospital.*

PREDICATE ADJECTIVE, PREDICATE NOUN

An adjective that completes—serves as complement of—a linking, or copulative, verb is classified as a predicate adjective. A noun that completes a linking verb is called a predicate noun or a predicate nominative.

- Everyone is *content* with the decision. (Predicate adjective *content* completes linking verb *is*.)
- The children seem *unhappy*, but their parents do not know why. (Predicate adjective *unhappy* completes linking verb *seem*.)
- Even totally uninformed people are *experts* when a discussion turns to foreign affairs or taxation. (Predicate noun *experts* completes linking verb *are*.)
- You become a qualified *mechanic* only after a year of training and at least two years of supervised experience. (Predicate noun *mechanic* completes linking verb *become*.)

PREFIX

A prefix is a unit of one or more letters or syllables added to the beginning of a stem or word to form another word. Several dozen prefixes are commonly used in English. A few of them are *a*, as in amoral; *sub*, as in subordinate; *pan*, as in pantheism; *poly*, as in polytheism; and *in*, as in inborn.

Suffixes are syllables added to the ends of words. Together, prefixes and suffixes are called *affixes*.

PREPOSITIONS AND PREPOSITIONAL PHRASES

Prepositions

A preposition shows the relationship of a noun or pronoun to another element in a sentence.

- *to* the *theater* (preposition *to*, object of preposition *theater*)
- *on* the highest *limb* (preposition *on*, object of preposition *limb*)
- *with* the utmost *ease* (preposition *with*, object of preposition *ease*)
- *across* the wide *part of* the *river* (preposition *across*, object of preposition *part*; preposition *of*, object of preposition *river*)

Preposition Problems

Excessive use of prepositions can mar a sentence:

Clumsy For what reason did you ask her *to* let you read *to* her *from* the book? (Four prepositions clutter this sentence. Notice that the second *to* is part of the infinitive *to let*. Even though the use of *to* with the infinitive *let* requires that *to* be classified as a *function word*, it is nevertheless read as a preposition.)

Improved Why did you offer *to* read *from* the book?

Clumsy With so little time left *to* make preparations *in case of* fire, we still have *to* get *in out of* the sunshine and get *to* work.

Improved So little time remains *to* install proper fire protection that we must begin now.

Prepositions at the ends of sentences disturb many teachers of English—generally teachers who have not kept their stylistic eyes and ears open in recent years.

- In her extreme distress, she had no one to turn *to*. (To satisfy a fussy teacher, we may write *she had no one to whom to turn*, but good sense will tell us not to write anything that clumsy once we are free of that teacher.)
- He had no one to play *with*. (*He had no one with whom to play* may satisfy a purist, but we must never fall prey to a barbarism such as: *He had no one with whom to play with*.)

We all have been told not to end a sentence with a preposition, yet English idiom and rhythm frequently demand disobedience. Even so, the controversy persists. To conclude the discussion, consider a quatrain written by the American poet Berton Braley in the 19th century:

The grammar has a rule absurd
Which I would call an outworn myth:
"A preposition is a word
You mustn't end a sentence with!"

Prepositional Phrases

A prepositional phrase consists of a preposition, the object of the preposition, and any modifiers of the object. Prepositional phrases are among the most widely used modifying structures in the language.

- They suffered deeply *during the Holocaust*. (The verb *suffered* is modified by the adverb *deeply* and by the prepositional phrase *during the Holocaust*.)
- Give me the details *after dinner*. (The verb *give* is modified by the prepositional phrase *after dinner*.)

Writers have little trouble in using prepositional phrases unless (1) questions of diction arise—different *from* or different *than*?—or (2) bulky prepositions are used in great numbers—*in regard to*, *in case of*, and many others.

General and formal usage prefer *different from*:

- French Canadians are *different from* English Canadians in many ways. (An improved form of this sentence is *French Canadians differ from English Canadians in many ways*.)
- Their ambitions are *different from* ours. (This sentence may also be written as *Their ambitions* differ from *ours*.)

PRINCIPAL, PRINCIPLE

If you cannot remember the spelling of these two words, you are not alone. Confusion of *principal* and *principle* has reached epidemic proportions.

First for some of the exceptions: a *principal* is a leading member of a cast or an acting company (probably because a star performer once was called *principal singer*, *principal actor*, or the like); head of a school (probably because a principal once was the *principal teacher* in a school); a capital sum, the *principal*, distinct from interest or profit; and *principals* own most of the stock in a company (probably because they once were *principal participants*).

Except for such uses, *principal* is an adjective, and *principle* is a noun.

- Our *principal* complaint is that the group seemed to have no *principles*. (The adjective *principal* modifies *complaint*. The noun *principles* (guiding tenets) functions as the direct object of the infinitive *have*.)

- The *principal* witness in the case said she was not concerned with the interest, but cared only about the *principal*. (The adjective *principal* modifies *complaint*. The noun *principal* (sum of money) functions as the object of the preposition *about*.)

PRINCIPAL PARTS OF A VERB

The principal parts of a verb are the forms from which all other forms derive: infinitive, past, and past participle. (We sometimes consider the present participle the fourth principal part of a verb.)

Regular, or weak, verbs form the past and past participle by adding *ed* to the infinitive: *walk, walked, walked; love, loved, loved*. By adding auxiliary verbs, we can form all the tenses: *will walk, have walked, will have walked*, etc.

Irregular, or strong, verbs form the past and past participle by a vowel change, or by no change at all in at least one case: *bid, bid, bid* (in the sense of *offer*).

Here are some of the most common strong verbs:

begin	began	begun
blow	blew	blown
bring	brought	brought
choose	chose	chosen
come	came	come
dive	dived (*also* dove)	dived
do	did	done
draw	drew	drawn
drink	drank	drunk
fly	flew	flown
forget	forgot	forgotten (*also* forgot)
freeze	froze	frozen
get	got	got (*also* gotten)
go	went	gone
know	knew	known
lie	lay	lain
ride	rode	ridden
ring	rang (*also* rung)	rung
rise	rose	risen

run	ran	run
see	saw	seen
shrink	shrank (*also* shrunk)	shrunk
sing	sang (*also* sung)	sung
spring	sprang (*also* sprung)	sprung
swim	swam	swum
swing	swung	swung
take	took	taken
throw	threw	thrown
write	wrote	written

If you are unsure of the principal parts of any verb, consult your dictionary.

PROFESSOR

A person with the academic rank of assistant professor or above should be addressed as *Professor* in an academic setting. This practice is followed in writing letters other than personal letters. Use the abbreviation *Prof.* when writing out the full name; spell the word out when using the last name alone.

- Prof. Andrew L. Eastwood
- Professor Eastwood

In giving the full title of a professor, specify the person's professorial rank.

- Andrew L. Eastwood, Associate Professor of Oriental Languages and Literature

Since *professor* is an indication of rank, the term should not be applied to faculty members who are not professors. Before the name of a teacher who is below professorial rank, use *Mr., Mrs., Miss,* or *Ms.* If the teacher has a doctor's degree, use *Dr.*

PROGRESSIVE VERBS

Progressive verbs are formed by the present participle and the appropriate form of the verb *be.* A progressive verb indicates that the action described is in progress at the time specified or understood.

Verbs in the various progressive tenses are shown in the following examples. Voice is also indicated.

- He *is walking* the dog now. (present progressive active)
- The dog *is being walked* now. (present progressive passive).

PRONOUNS

- He *was walking* the dog when you called. (past progressive active)
- The dog *was being walked* when you called. (past progressive passive)
- I *have been walking* for three hours. (present perfect progressive active)
- He *had been walking* the dog for over an hour when the car appeared. (past perfect progressive active)
- I *will be walking* as soon as I complete this call. (future progressive active)
- He *will have been walking* the dog for over an hour and will be too tired to stop for a chat. (future perfect progressive active)

PRONOUNS

Pronouns are words that take the place of nouns and perform all noun functions. They create difficulty because many of them have different forms in the subjective, objective, and possessive cases, and strong conventions exist for the use of these cases in certain constructions.

Personal Pronouns

Personal pronouns have different forms for the subjective, possessive, and objective cases.

	Subjective	*Possessive*	*Objective*
First Person			
Singular	I	mine	me
Plural	we	ours	us
Second Person			
Singular	you	yours	you
Plural	you	yours	you
Third Person			
Singular	he, she, it	his, hers, its	him, her, it
Plural	they	theirs	them

The examples that follow illustrate pronouns in the possessive case as well as possessive adjectives. This is done to show how possessive pronouns differ from possessive adjectives.

Pronoun I tell you that *mine* is best. (The possessive pronoun *mine* functions as subject of *is*.)

Adjective My motorcycle costs much more than *your* bicycle. (Two possessive adjectives: *my* modifies *motorcycle*; *your* modifies

132

bicycle.)

Pronoun Yours has been selected. (possessive pronoun)

Adjective Your prose style has improved. (possessive adjective)

Pronoun Theirs does not perform as well as *hers.* (two possessive pronouns)

Adjective Their reference shelf is much more valuable than *your* one-volume encyclopedia. (two possessive adjectives)

In the preceding examples the possessive pronouns *mine, yours, theirs,* and *hers* perform noun functions. The possessive adjectives *my, your,* and *their* function as modifiers.

Relative Pronouns

Relative pronouns—*who, whom, which, what, whoever, whomever, whichever, whatever,* and *that*—are used to introduce subordinate clauses. The forms of relative pronouns may cause difficulties for writers, particularly when a relative pronoun functions as object of a preposition.

Correct The boy *whom* you gave the bicycle *to* does not want it.

Correct The boy *to whom* you gave the bicycle does not want it.

Incorrect The boy *who* you gave the bicycle *to* does not want it.
  (While teachers and editors would consider the pronoun *who* wrong in this sentence, it is commonly heard in colloquial speech. The sentence is also given as *The boy you gave the bicycle to does not want it.*)

Subjective	Possessive	Objective
who	whose	whom
that	(*no form*)	that
which	whose	which
what	(*no form*)	what
whoever	whosever	whomever
whichever	(*no form*)	whichever

Reflexive Pronouns

Pronouns combined with *self* are termed reflexive. They refer to the pronoun or noun that functions as subject of a verb and are used to give emphasis to the pronoun or noun.

- I will do it *myself.* (The reflexive pronoun *myself* refers to the pronoun *I.*)
- Gerald and I do things *ourselves.* (The reflexive pronoun *our-*

selves refers to the subject, *Gerald and I*.)
- You *yourself* will have to do this.
- You do things *yourselves*.
- She does things *herself*.
- They *themselves* do not know.

Demonstrative Pronouns

Demonstrative pronouns single out or indicate the person or thing to which they refer.

- *This* is no longer interesting when the child reaches five.
- *That* will satisfy my coach.

Other Pronouns

Three other types of pronouns merit mention: interrogative pronouns—*who, which, what*; indefinite pronouns—*any, anyone, some, someone*, etc.; and reciprocal pronouns—*each other, one another*.

PROOFREADING

Proofreading is the last essential step in preparing a manuscript. Before submitting a paper to an instructor or editor, be sure to read slowly through the complete manuscript, checking for correctness of spelling, pagination, and the like. Since every page is important, be sure to read the entire manuscript. For example, inconsistencies of form are commonly found in footnotes and bibliographies. When you consider how much time goes into writing and researching term papers and reports, surely the extra time needed for proofreading is a small expenditure.

PUBLIC

Public is a collective noun that takes either a singular or plural verb, depending on whether the word is intended as a single unit or as a collection of people.

- The public *is* often impatient for change.
- The public *are* often depicted as aggregations of power groups.

This same reasoning holds true in determining the number of all collective nouns.

PUNCTUATION

Two common misconceptions of beginning writers are that punctuation is entirely a matter of taste, and punctuation is determined by breath control. As a matter of fact, while there is some room for art in punctuating, specific rules govern most uses of the marks of punctuation. To make certain that your writing conforms to existing rules, check the entries in this book for each mark of punctuation and try to learn the rules as you read so that you will not have to check again and again and again.

Q

QUESTION MARK

A question mark (?) is used at the end of a sentence that asks a question.

- Will you go home for the holidays?
- Did the boy really ask for more?
- Are there any games left in the schedule?

If a sentence asking a question contains a quotation, the question mark is placed outside the final quotation mark; if the quotation is itself a question, the question mark falls inside the final quotation mark.

- Are you certain you did not say, "Other students participated in the demonstration just for kicks"? (The sentence asks a question.)
- He said, "Is there any doubt that the entire group was at fault?" (The sentence does not ask a question. The quotation is a question.)

A question mark is also used to indicate that a date is uncertain.

- Julian of Norwich, born 1342(?), was a recluse in a cell attached to the Church of St. Julian at Norwich.
- Archimedes (287?–212 B.C.)

QUESTIONS

We normally use inverted word order in a sentence that asks a question: *Were you* late yesterday? (Subject *you* follows verb *were*.) Inverted order is also used when auxiliary verbs are part of the verb.

- *Can you meet* the class tomorrow?
- *Have you* any wool?
- *Will you wait* for me?

Notice that certain questions can also be expressed in normal word order:

- *You drink* beer after dinner?
- *He* really *said* that he was unable to attend?

This word order is more appropriate to speech than to writing, but it can appear in writing when questions are being quoted verbatim.

QUOTATION MARKS

Quotation marks are used most frequently to indicate that the material enclosed within them is quoted directly from another source. When a quotation appears within a quotation, single quotation marks are used for the internal quotation. Normally, single and double quotation marks are placed outside the final punctuation of the quotation. When single and double quotation marks occur together, both are placed outside the final punctuation of the quotation: "Writing to his friend William Erskine in 1796, Sir Walter Scott noted that many apologies for publication 'are in fact no apologies at all. Either the things are worth the attention of the public or they are not.' "
—Sir Walter Scott, *Life of John Dryden,* Ed. Bernard Kreissman, (University of Nebraska Press, 1963), p. vii.

Extensive Quotation

When the quoted material is extensive—one rule of thumb is five typewritten lines or more—it is set off from the rest of the paper. An extensive quotation is single spaced, indented, and not enclosed in quotation marks.

> Now, for the first time since the end of World War II, we may be approaching a point from which it will be possible to see the shape of a new European order to replace the system that was destroyed so blindly fifty years ago; it is perhaps not too much to say that the lights which went out for Sir Edward Grey in 1914 are flickering on again. At present the process of reconciliation between the two Europes is proceeding without effective American participation because of America's preoccupation with the Vietnamese war; the result of course is that the United States is being left behind and Western Europe's developing friendliness with Eastern Europe is beginning to separate Europe from America.
>
> —J. William Fulbright, *The Arrogance of Power,* (New York, 1966), p. 216.

Dialogue

Dialogue is enclosed in quotation marks. Every time the speaker changes, a new paragraph is required.
"Who is it, Jessie?"
"No one you know, Mom."

When the speaker is indicated, a comma or two commas are used in addition to the quotation marks.

- Maria said, "Half the trouble could have been averted if the authorities had arrived promptly." (indication of speaker before quotation)
- "Half the trouble could have been averted," Maria said, "if the authorities had arrived promptly." (indication of speaker within quotation)
- "Half the trouble could have been averted if the authorities had arrived promptly," Maria said. (indication of speaker after quotation)

Notice that *if* is not capitalized in the second example, since it is part of the sentence being quoted.

Titles

Quotation marks are used for the titles of works contained within other works—individual stories in a collection of short stories, magazine articles, chapters of a book, titles of poems in a collection of poetry—and for song titles.

- "The Gambler, the Nun, and the Radio," from *The Fifth Column and the First Forty-Nine Stories*
- "Yes and No," from *Selected Poems and Parodies*
- "John Henry," from *American Ballads and Folk Songs*

Notice that the title of the larger work—from which the shorter work is cited—is printed in italics. In typewritten or handwritten papers, underscoring indicates that italics would be used in print.

Words Used as Words

Quotation marks may be used to indicate that a word is used as a word rather than to convey the meaning of the word. Italics are also used for this purpose.

- You have consistently employed "effect" where "affect" is the correct term. (The two words enclosed in quotation marks are not used to convey the meanings of those words. The quotation marks make it clear that "effect" and "affect" are used as words.)

Apologetic Quotation Marks

Many writers follow the practice of enclosing an inappropriate word or phrase in quotation marks, thinking that by doing so they will make the element appropriate. The use of so-called apologetic quotation marks is not acceptable in formal writing.

- The champion "demolished" his opponent in the final game. (The writer may be trying to indicate either that *demolished* is not to be taken literally or to apologize for using a word in the sense intended. If the context makes it clear that *demolished* is not to be taken literally, no apology is needed. If the writer considers this use of *demolished* inappropriate, the word should be replaced.)

It is far better to find words that express the writer's intentions precisely and do so without apology. Using quotation marks around words cannot be counted on to make clear to the reader just what is intended by the writer.

R

REAL, REALLY

Real is an adjective, and *really* is an adverb. In informal English, *real* is often used as an adverb: You look *real* well. He is a *real* good guy. Such usage is not acceptable in papers written in general or formal English except when the word is part of material being quoted from the speech of someone who uses informal English.

REASON IS BECAUSE

After the construction *the reason is* or *was* and the like, general and formal English require either a noun or a noun clause introduced by *that*. *The reason is because* is common in colloquial speech, but unacceptable in writing.

- The reason is *that his mother will not let him apply*. (noun clause completing linking verb *is*)
- The explanation for his defeat was the indignant *response* he had from most voters. (noun *response* completing the linking verb *was*)

REFERENCE OF POSSESSIVE ADJECTIVES AND PRONOUNS

Faulty reference of pronouns and possessive adjectives is one of the most common grammatical errors. The problem takes two forms—either a pronoun or possessive adjective does not agree in number with its referent, or a pronoun or possessive adjective has no clearly visible referent.

Possessive Adjectives

Unacceptable White America, during *its* westward expansion and claiming *their* actions were furthering the process of civilization, denied Native Americans the freedom to roam their land. (The writer of this sentence apparently could not decide whether *White America* should be plural or singular. The result of the indecision was a compromise—the first possessive adjective is singular; the second is plural.)

Improved White America, during the westward expansion and claiming *its* actions were furthering the process of civilization,

140

denied Native Americans the freedom to roam their land. (One of the possessive adjectives in the original sentence has been eliminated. The other, *their*, has been changed to *its*.)

Unacceptable Unless White America accepts African American equality and does not restrain *their* freedom, we shall not see peace in this generation. (What is the referent of *their*? One would suppose the writer meant *African Americans*, but that term does not appear in the sentence.)

Improved Unless White America accepts the equality of African Americans and does not restrain *their* freedom, we shall not see peace in this generation. (The plural possessive adjective *their* now has a plural referent, *African Americans*.)

Pronouns

Poor The *technique* is called extended imagery because *it uses words* that are carried from one sentence to another. (The pronoun *it* appears to have *technique* as its antecedent, but one cannot say that a technique *uses words*.)

Improved The technique is called extended imagery, because *the writer uses* words that are carried from one sentence to another. (The pronoun *it* has been replaced by *the writer*. The pronoun problem is solved.)

Improved The technique is called extended imagery, because *it* is characterized by the use of words carried from one sentence to another. (Now the pronoun *it*, with the antecedent *technique*, is no longer said to be using anything. Instead *it* is correctly employed as the subject of *is characterized*.)

Improved In the technique called extended imagery, words are carried from one sentence to another. (Not a pronoun in sight, and the sentence is as clear as can be.)

The best way to avoid the problem of faulty reference of possessive adjectives and pronouns is to edit your work carefully. Take special care to determine whether all possessive adjectives and pronouns have correct referents and whether possessive adjectives and pronouns are in the correct number. In addition, make certain that these troublesome elements are close to the word or words to which they refer.

RELATIVE PRONOUN

Relative pronouns can refer to people, objects, and animals. The relative pronouns are *who*, *whom*, *that*, and *which*. When *who*, *whom*, or *which* is combined with *-ever* or *-soever*, the resulting form is also classified as a relative pronoun.

Relative pronouns are used to introduce relative clauses—subordinate clauses that modify an antecedent.

- The woman *who talked to the Lions Club* is a friend of mine. (The relative clause, introduced by the relative pronoun *who*, modifies *woman*.)
- There stood the sculpture *that I had made*. (The relative clause, introduced by the relative pronoun *that*, modifies *sculpture*.)
- There stood the sculpture *I had made*. (The relative clause without the relative pronoun *that*. It is often possible to delete the relative pronouns *that* and *whom*.)
- He is the person *whom I saw on the train*. (The relative clause, introduced by the relative pronoun *whom*, modifies *person*.)
- He is the person *I saw on the train*. (The relative clause without the relative pronoun *whom*.)

REPETITION

Teachers of writing try to make clear to their students that repetition is not always a characteristic of poor style. Indeed, a good stylist fastens on the precise word or expression needed to express an important thought in a piece of writing and then uses it as often as appropriate.

While teachers may encourage the use of a thesaurus to avoid unnecessary repetition, some students mistakenly take this suggestion to mean that they must never use the same word twice within a piece of writing. With the many choices a thesaurus provides, the students may neglect to consult a dictionary to check the interesting terms they find. The result is that they find—and use—synonyms that are inappropriate in context.

Awkward Repetition

Repetition is awkward when it is unnecessary, when it does not provide emphasis, or when it does not add to meaning.

Awkward *It is through imagery* that most poets convey meaning; *it is through* this *imagery* that the reader must discover meaning. (The awkward repetition of *it is through*—not a particularly striking phrase—emphasizes something that is not worth emphasizing and does not add to meaning. The repetition of *imagery*, although an important word, is not necessary in so short a sentence. Since these repetitions appear to add words and achieve nothing more, the sentence should be edited severely.)

Improved Poets convey *meaning* through imagery, and readers must discover *meaning* there. (The noun *meaning*, an important word in this sentence, is repeated primarily because substitution of the pronoun *it* would result in ambiguity—would the antecedent of *it* be *meaning* or *imagery*? Try substituting *it* in the improved sentence to decide for yourself. By repeating *meaning*, the pronoun problem disappears, and *meaning* is emphasized—a double benefit.)

Examine the following excerpt from a student paper on Tolstoy's novel *The Death of Ivan Ilyich*. Notice the awkward repetition of *phony*, which is an inappropriate word to use in formal writing:

Ivan's awareness is, in essence, his dissatisfaction with his past life. The first sign of this awareness, that man is a phony, occurs when Ivan consults his physician about his illness. Ivan also recognizes his wife and daughter as phonies when they discuss his health. This is in contrast with the pure Gerasim, who is not a phony but a real and sympathetic person.

The main problem with such writing is that the reader is attracted to the awkward repetition of *phony* rather than to what the writer is saying. The reader finds it difficult to focus on the thought advanced because of the language employed by the writer.

By way of contrast, examine two examples of repetition that increase understanding and heighten stylistic effectiveness:

- Victory at all costs, victory in spite of all terror, victory however long and hard the road may be; for without victory there is no survival. (The most striking word in this sentence, of course, is *victory*. By repeating it so often, the writer has driven home the central thought.)
- We shall fight on the beaches, we shall fight on the landing grounds, we shall fight in the fields and in the streets, we shall fight in the hills; we shall never surrender. (You can be certain *we shall fight*. Repetition has done its job.)

Both these famous sentences of Winston Churchill illustrate the importance of intentional repetition of important thoughts expressed identically each time. Repetition is effective when thoughts are worth emphasizing, awkward when they are not.

RESTRICTIVE, NONRESTRICTIVE

A restrictive modifier limits the sentence element modified; a nonrestrictive modifier adds information that is not essential for limiting the sentence element modified. Restrictive modifiers—vital to the meaning of the sentence—are not set off by punctuation; nonrestrictive modifiers—not vital to meaning—are set off by commas.

Restrictive The man *who told the story* is my father. (The modifier *who told the story* is restrictive—vital to the meaning of the sentence—since without it there is no identification of the *man* under discussion: The man is my father. What man? The man *who told the story*. Since the modifier *who told the story* is restrictive, commas are not used to set it off.)

Nonrestrictive My father, *the man who told the story*, has lived in this area for many years. (In this sentence the main statement stands without the modifier *the man who told the story*: *My father has lived in this area for many years*. The key to identifying *father*, the subject of the sentence, is the possessive adjective *my*. Once we have that word, *father* is completely identified, and any further modification is nonrestrictive. As a nonrestrictive modifier, *the man who told the story* must be set off by commas in the sentence in which it appears.)

Examine the following examples, both punctuated correctly:

Restrictive **1.** Two reporters *who covered the crime story* were nationally known. (Take note that commas do not set off the restrictive modifier *who covered the crime story* in this sentence.)

Nonrestrictive **2.** Seth Johnson and Carl Weber, *two reporters who covered the crime story*, were nationally known. (The nonrestrictive modifier *two reporters who covered the crime story* is set off by commas in this sentence.)

In example 1, since there are more than two reporters who are nationally known, the clause *who covered the crime story* limits *reporters*.

In example 2, only two men who are nationally known may be presumed to be named Seth Johnson and Carl Weber. Additional identification, for instance, *two reporters who covered the crime story*, does not limit *reporters* further.

Once a name appears in a sentence, further modification is usually nonrestrictive. The exception occurs when a name is so common that further identification is required: *John Smith, William Brown,* and the like.

The examples given so far have been of restrictive and nonrestrictive *clauses,* but modifying *phrases* are also classified in this way and observe the same rules of punctuation.

- Henry the Eighth, *King of England,* married more than once. (nonrestrictive)
- Mersault, *the main character in Camus' novel,* appeared totally detached from life. (nonrestrictive)
- The man *flying the kite* tripped and fell. (restrictive)
- The house *across the street* is for sale. (restrictive)

In the first two sentences, the modifiers are enclosed in commas, indicating that they are nonrestrictive. In the next two sentences, the absence of commas tells us that the modifiers are restrictive.

RHETORIC

In the context of this book, the term *rhetoric* may be defined as the art of using language, both oral and written. *Rhetoric* has additional definitions, including one that is disparaging, as intended in a sentence such as "What has been said by my opponent is only rhetoric." This sentence is the equivalent of "Words, empty words."

RHETORICAL QUESTION

A rhetorical question is one for which no answer is expected. A rhetorical question may be thought as a statement in the form of a question. In conversation, rhetorical questions are often mocking in tone:

- If you know so much, why didn't you answer the question? (Translation: You are ignorant.)
- How could you have done that? (Translation: You have made a terrible mistake.)
- Are you really foolhardy enough to go over the falls without a life jacket? (Translation: You would be foolish to do so.)

In exposition, rhetorical questions may serve a useful purpose. While no reply to the questions is called for, the reader is expected to accept the argument of the person posing them.

> Has he not also another object, which is that they may be impoverished by payment of taxes and thus compelled to devote themselves to their daily wants and therefore less likely to conspire against him?

> —Plato, *Republic*

In asking this question, Plato implants the suspicion that taxation has a motive other than support of the legitimate functions of the republic. The question is not to be answered, and Plato's statement has had its effect.

Rhetorical questions also serve as a good way to introduce a topic for consideration. Read this series of rhetorical questions posed in a textbook to open a discussion of how to listen effectively:

How would you like to sit down now at a lecture for college seniors on the geological history of Outer Mongolia? How much would you learn from it—assuming you have not studied the topic previously? How could you possibly take notes when everything the lecturer says is new as far as you are concerned? (The stage is set for the discussion of *listening* that follows.)

Such uses of rhetorical questions must not be overlooked in writing college papers. One word of warning: The effectiveness of this device—or any other rhetorical device—can be dissipated quickly if overused.

S

SCHWA

(ə) is the symbol used in the International Phonetic Alphabet to represent an unstressed vowel, for example, nick*e*l, *a*board, inf*i*nite. In the IPA the italicized vowels in these words are replaced by the schwa.

SEASONS

The names of the seasons are not capitalized except in some poetry and poetic prose.

SELF

Intensive and reflexive pronouns are formed by adding *self* to the base form. As an intensive, the pronoun is used for emphasis: He *himself* will do it. As a reflexive, the pronoun frequently occupies the object position: Please *yourself* by doing what you want.

As a prefix, *self* is joined to the root word by a hyphen: self-control, self-made, self-oriented, self-starting. When *self* is the root word, no hyphen is used: selfish, selfless, selfsame.

SEMICOLON

The semicolon has two principal uses in a sentence. It may connect two or more independent clauses when a coordinating conjunction is not used, and it may separate the elements of an internally punctuated series.

Independent Clauses

When no close relationship exists between independent clauses, a semicolon may be used to connect them.

- He raced off as fast as he could; we followed at a leisurely pace.
- The trip had been interesting and enjoyable; all of us were content.

A semicolon may be used along with a conjunctive adverb to join independent clauses when a close relationship exists between the two clauses.

- The air was turbulent and the storm severe; *nevertheless*, no one seemed unduly worried. (Notice the semicolon before the conjunctive adverb and the comma that follows it.)

- The politics of today bears little relationship to what we knew years ago; *however*, there is no doubt that the old political loyalties lie dormant. (semicolon before, comma after)

Internally Punctuated Series

When even one element of a series is internally punctuated, semicolons are used to separate the elements from one another.

- Consider the burden imposed by modern taxation: road taxes, which are imposed on all vehicles going through the town; import and export taxes; income taxes; and sales taxes. (The first element of the series has an internal comma, so semicolons are used between elements.)

When no element of a series is internally punctuated, commas between elements suffice. Although many newspapers and magazines have a tendency to omit the comma before the final element in a series, in formal papers this comma is retained.

- The prospectus included the title, publisher, cost, detailed description of the program, and list of all required materials.
- We help newcomers stay out of trouble by offering three suggestions: never criticize strangers, avoid sarcasm, and mind your own business.

SHALL, WILL

The distinctions formerly observed between the uses of *shall* and *will* as auxiliary verbs in the simple future indicative have all but disappeared. Current practice in formal writing is to use *shall* in the first person singular and plural, *will* in the second and third persons. In speech, and in general and informal writing, *will* is used in all persons.

Formal I *shall* eat my dinner now, if I may.
We *shall* eat our dinner now.
You *will* find me at home after seven.
She (he, they) *will* surely lose the way.

Informal I (we, you, they) will eat now.

In questions, *shall* is frequently used in the first and third persons, *will* in the second person.

- *Shall* I go? What *shall* we do? What *will* I (we) do?

- *Will* you help us?
- *Shall* the child be permitted to go? (*Will* the children be allowed to go?

SHOULD, WOULD

Should and *would*—originally past forms of *shall* and *will*—now have several special meanings:

1. *Should* suggests obligation, though somewhat weaker than *ought*.

- I *should* get the report done, I suppose.
- I really *ought to* get the report done. (Notice the inclusion of *to* after *ought*.)
- He felt that he *should* oblige her, since she had been so kind.
- You may not wish to pay the entire bill, but you *ought to* pay your share.

2. *Should* conveys a sense of uncertainty.

- The package *should* be delivered by noon if all goes well.
- The ship *should* arrive on time, weather permitting.

3. *Should* and *would* are used to state polite requests: in formal usage, *should* is used in the first person, *would* in the second and third. Usage is divided, however, and many authorities feel that *would* may be used in all persons.

- I *should* like to explain my position on this matter.
- I *would* like to explain my position on this matter.
- *Would* you please explain your position on this matter?
- *Would* the witness please explain her position on this matter?

SIC

A word from Latin, meaning "thus." Enclosed in brackets, *sic* is used to indicate an error in quoted material.

- "They hoped to develope [*sic*] three more products."
- Many officials who should know better continue to refer to "nucular [*sic*] war."

SLANG

Slang expressions appear in English as long as the language continues to grow. Occupational groups—sportswriters, engineers, teachers, musicians, and many others—employ specialized jargon to describe the thoughts, facts, and events they must deal with over and over again. Searching for freshness of expression, members of such groups constantly add to the store of jargon. When their audiences employ jargon for their own use, it is classified first as slang and later as informal language. Eventually, some of it appears in formal English. Cultural and ethnic subgroups develop their own argot, and much of that also moves into informal, and sometimes formal, language.

This ongoing manufacture of new words and expressions—and new meanings for existing words and expressions—may mark users as *with it* (slang for *knowledgable*.) Most slang dies a worthy death: *23 skidoo* for the once slang, now informal *beat it*, and *wooden kimono* for *coffin*. Other slang expressions persist over long periods until they are in general use and become absorbed into the language: *sharp*, informal for *very stylish*; *cop*, informal, (but not *fuzz*, which is still considered slang) for *police officer*; *hot dog*; *O.K.*; and many others.

Slang is best avoided in writing, but it can be used in dialogue if the character speaking would naturally use slang. When you employ a slang expression appropriately, do not enclose it in quotation marks. If the expression is right for your purposes, there is no need to apologize; if it is wrong, quotation marks will not get you off the hook. (See QUOTATION MARKS.)

SLOW, SLOWLY

Slow was once clearly an adjective and *slowly* an adverb, but this distinction is breaking down. One commonly observes road signs exhorting motorists to *DRIVE SLOW* and hears fathers imploring their sons to *drive slow* and *stop quick* in case of trouble. The formal language still retains this grammatical distinction: *drive slowly*, *stop quickly*.

SO

So is both a conjunction and an intensifier. As an intensifier, *so* is rarely used in formal English.

Intensifier

Informal The painting was *so* beautiful. (The intensifier is a vague replacement for the equally vague intensifier *very*.)

Formal The painting was *extraordinarily* beautiful. (Now the sentence appears to say something more than *so* or *very*, implying an order of magnitude more than *beautiful*. But we still don't know much about the beauty of the painting.)

Formal Imaginative brushwork and boldness of color in that beautiful painting set it apart from all the others in the gallery. (Specific information is supplied, perhaps enabling the reader to understand the empty claims made in the other versions of the sentence.)

Conjunction

As a conjunction, *so* is used to introduce clauses of purpose or result.

- Most mourners stood apart from the members of the bereaved family *so* they would not appear to be violating the family's privacy. (clause of purpose)
- Ernest's reviews became increasingly vitriolic, *so* he was dismissed. (clause of result)

In formal writing, *so* is often followed by *that*.

- Booksellers decided to give less rack space to novels *so that* their profits would increase.
- He left early *so that* he could get a good seat.

In general writing, *that* is frequently omitted after *so*.

- Booksellers decided to give less rack space to novels *so* their profits would increase.
- He left early *so* he could get a good seat.

SOME

Some is used both as an adjective and as an indefinite pronoun. As an adjective, the word presents no problem for writers; as an indefinite pronoun, it can be worrisome.

- *Some* guests do insist on leaving late. (adjective modifying *guests*)
- *Some* insist on leaving late. (indefinite pronoun functioning as subject of *insist*)
- He ate *some* nuts and left the rest. (adjective modifying *nuts*)
- He ate *some* and left *some*. (indefinite pronouns functioning as objects of *ate* and *left* respectively)

Sentences employing *some* as pronoun may depend for their meaning on preceding sentences. If the antecedents are clear enough, the pronoun does not cause a problem. When an antecedent is not clear enough, the sentence must be revised.

Ambiguous Republicans and Democrats were equally enthusiastic about the qualifications of the candidate, but *some* were not willing to cross party lines to vote for her. (Some Democrats or some Republicans? If previous sentences have identified the candidate as a member of one of the political parties, we have a chance of understanding whether *some* refers to *Republicans* or *Democrats*. If previous sentences have not identified the party affiliation of the candidate, we need a divining rod.)

Revised Both parties were enthusiastic about the Republican candidate, but the Democrats were reluctant to cross party lines to vote for her.

All compounds of *some* are written as one word: *someone, somebody, something, somewhere, somewhat.* If *some* is unusually stressed, it maintains its status as a separate word: *some one, some body, some thing,* but not *some where* or *some what.*

SPELLING

The following list contains words frequently misspelled by the unwary. The best way to use the list to improve your spelling is to have someone quiz you on the words that give you trouble. Place each word you miss on a flash card and review all your cards until you have the spellings firmly in mind. The dictionary is used over and over again by poor spellers, who have to look some words up every time they use them. If you are one of these unfortunates, you can reduce the number of words you have to look up and save time that can be used to improve the quality of your writing.

Spelling List

absence	acquainted	aggression
absorption	across	aisle
accept	additionally	allege
acceptance	addressed	allotment
access	admirable	all right
accessible	advice	allusion
accidentally	advisable	allusive
accommodate	advise	altar
accumulate	adviser (*also*	alter
accustom	advisor)	altogether
achievement	affect	amateur
achiever	aggravate	analogous

analysis	Britain	control
analyze	bureau	convenience
angel	calendar	coolly
angelic	candidate	cooperate
angelically	canvas	cooperative
angle	canvass	council
annual	capital	councilor
annually	capitol	counselor
anxiety	carburetor	courageous
anyone (*also*	casually	courteous
any one)	category	courtesy
apologetically	cemetery	deceit
apology	changeable	deceive
apparatus	chaperon	decision
apparent	chaperone	declared
appearance	characteristic	defendant
appreciate	characteristically	deferred
appropriate	chauffeur	definite
arctic	choose	dependence
arguing	chose	descend
arouse	clothes	descendant
ascend	colonel	describing
assassin	colossal	desert
athletic	committee	desiccate
athletically	comparative	desirable
attacked	compatible	desiring
attendance	compel	desperate
audience	complement	dessert
bachelor	compliment	dictionary
balance	concede	difference
battalion	conceive	dining
belief	connoisseur	diphtheria
believe	conquer	disappear
beneficial	conqueror	disappoint
benefited	conscience	disastrous
benefiting	conscientious	disease
boundary	consensus	disparate
breakdown	contemptible	dispatch
bridal	contemptibly	dissipate
bridle	continuous	distribute

divine
dormitories
dramatically
dripped
dripping
dropped
dropping
each other
ecstasy
eighth
embarrass
emphatically
enforce
environment
equipment
equipped
especially
everyday (*also*
every day)
exaggerate
exceed
excellence
except
exhaust
exhilarate
existence
expense
experience
facility
familiar
fascinate
fatal
fault
feasible
February
feebly
fiery
financier
forehead
foreign

forfeit
formally
formerly
fourth
frantically
fraternity
friend
fundamental
furniture
genius
gently
ghost
gnaw
government
governor
grammar
grief
grievous
guarantee
guerrilla
guidance
handicapped
handkerchief
hangar
height
heinous
heroes
hindrance
human
humane
humorous
hypnotize
hypocrisy
hysterical
hysterically
imaginary
immediately
improvement
inadequate
incessantly

incidentally
incredible
indefiniteness
independence
indict
indispensable
indisputable
inflammation
influential
ingenious
ingenuous
initiate
innuendo
innumerable
inoculate
in order
intellectual
intelligence
intercede
interpretive
irrelevant
irreligious
irresistible
its
knew
knowledge
laboratory
legitimate
leisure
let's
liable
library
lieutenant
lightning
livelihood
loneliness
loose
lose
mackerel
magnificent

maintain
maintenance
manageable
manual
manufacturer
marital
marriage
mathematics
medicine
metal
mettle
miniature
mischievous
misspelled
misstatement
mortgage
murmur
muscle
mysterious
naive
necessary
negritude
nickel
nil
noticeable
notoriety
obedient
obstacle
occasion
occur
occurred
occurrence
occurring
omit
omitted
omitting
operate
opportunity
optimistic
outrageous

pamphlet
pantomime
parallel
parliament
participate
pastime
perform
permanence
permissible
perseverance
persistence
perspiration
persuade
Philippines
physical
physician
picnic
picnicking
playwright
pneumonia
politician
possess
possession
possibility
precede
precedent
preference
preferred
preferring
prejudice
presence
primitive
principal
principle
privilege
procedure
proceed
professor
program
pronunciation

propeller
protuberance
psychoanalyze
psychology
publicly
pumpkin
quantity
quiet
quite
quizzed
quizzes
quizzical
quizzing
receipt
receive
recommend
recurred
recurrence
recurring
reference
referendum
referred
referring
relevance
religion
Renaissance
repelled
repellent (*also* -ant)
repelling
repetition
resemblance
reservoir
respectfully
respectively
restaurant
rhyme
rhythm
ridiculous
sacrifice
sacrilegious

155

salary	strength	Tuesday
sandwich	subtle	typical
scene	subtly	typically
schedule	succeed	tyranny
scissors	success	underwent
secretary	successful	undoubtedly
seize	suite	unnatural
sensitive	superintendent	unnaturally
separate	supersede	unnecessarily
sergeant	suppress	unnecessary
severely	surprise	unnerving
siege	susceptible	unparalleled
sieve	syllable	unprecedented
similar	symbol	until
sincerely	symbolic	usually
soliloquy	symbolically	vacuum
somewhere	symmetrical	vengeance
sophisticated	symmetrically	villain
sophomore	temperament	visibility
sovereign	temperamental	warrant
specifically	temperamentally	warring
specimen	tendency	weather
stationary	than (*also* then)	Wednesday
stationery	their (*also* there)	weird
statue	thorough	were
stature	thousandths	where
statute	till	whether
stomach	too	women
stopped	tragedy	writing
stopping	tragically	yacht

SPLIT VERB FORMS

The rule cautioning against splitting infinitives is as old as many of the rules that lie in wait for writers and speakers of English. The reason usually given for observing this rule is that split verbs are not good style, which is no reason at all. Actually, if this so-called rule is to serve any useful purpose, it should not stop at infinitives. A useful rule is *Do not split any verb or verbal unless splitting improves comprehension.*

Poor Many generations of Americans *have* under the threat of real or imagined war *seen fit* to take up arms and fight. (The verb *have seen fit* has been torn asunder by a prepositional phrase comprising no fewer than eight words. A gifted speaker can give this sentence all the clarity it needs, but a reader may not be able to do so.)

Improved Under the threat of real or imagined war, many generations of Americans *have seen fit* to take up arms and fight. (The parts of the verb have been rejoined, and comprehension has been made easy.)

Poor Would you care *to*, if you have the time, *go* with me to the store? (This infinitive, split by a subordinate clause, should trigger an anxiety attack in the person who wrote it.)

Improved If you have the time, would you care *to go* to the store with me?

The matter of splitting verb forms, then, depends on how a writer splits them. If the interrupting element is long, splitting will not improve understanding. In most sentences, comprehension depends not on whether an infinitive is split by a single-word modifier, but on whether modifiers of all elements of a sentence are placed as closely as possible to the elements they modify.

Observe the improvement in clarity gained in the following sentence by making slight repairs and finding better positions for modifiers.

Poor He said that swimming *occasionally* gives him pleasure. (Does the writer intend *swimming occasionally* or *occasionally gives*? A modifier such as this one, which can be taken as applicable to the preceding element or to the following element, is sometimes called a *squinting modifier*—it looks both left and right at the same time.)

Improvement Occasional swimming, he said, gives him pleasure. (Only one interpretation is possible.)

Improvement He said he *occasionally* derives pleasure from swimming. (Only one interpretation is possible.)

SPOONFUL

Words such as *spoonful, cupful,* and *shovelful* form their plurals by adding *s*: *spoonfuls, cupfuls, shovelfuls*. These words are measures of quantity rather than numbers of spoons, cups, or shovels filled with something or other. To say *three spoons full of milk* would mean one has three full spoons waiting to be spilled. *Three spoonfuls* would be an appropriate expression for a recipe. In speech we hear *spoons full* and *spoonfuls* used willy-nilly, but the distinction between them should be retained in writing.

STYLE

Judgments of style are concerned with considering how well the words and patterns of words a writer uses contribute to the writer's purpose—whether, for example, to inform, convince, explain, intrigue, entertain, or inspire. George Orwell cited six rules for style that he felt would be helpful when a writer's instinct for choosing the precise word or the precise construction breaks down:

1. Never use a metaphor, simile, or other figure of speech which you are used to seeing in print.

2. Never use a long word where a short one will do.

3. If it is possible to cut a word out, always cut it out.

4. Never use the passive where you can use the active.

5. Never use a foreign phrase, a scientific word or a jargon word if you can think of an everyday English equivalent.

6. Break any of these rules sooner than say anything outright barbarous.

—George Orwell, *Politics and the English Language*

Orwell was writing about bureaucratic English, but his six rules apply to all language used as an instrument for expressing any thought. For Orwell, then, style meant aptness of expression in making a statement, and his rules help mightily in achieving clear expression.

No one can teach style in six easy lessons. Style is individual and goes deeply into the personality of the writer. What must be done is to encourage all writers to develop their own styles, and teachers can do no more or no less than point out aspects of a student's style that appear good—or bad—to the teacher.

Yet, if Orwell can give six rules for style, it is also worthwhile to give six pointers on style that the authors of this book try to follow:

1. Before you write, identify the audience you are writing for. This will give your writing direction, determine the appropriate level of diction, and help settle the question of how thoroughly you will discuss the subject you are writing about.

2. Try always to put the logical subject of every sentence in the subject position—this works handily with Orwell's fourth rule, the one that recommends using verbs in the active voice wherever possible.

3. Find the most precise verb for every sentence you write. Avoid verbs that require modifiers in order to approach the degree of precision you wish to achieve.

4. If you use figurative language, examine it to determine whether it is consistent and fresh and whether it adds to meaning.

5. Evaluate your diction. Is all your writing at the same appropriate level? Is it precise? Does it convey your intended meaning? Your dictionary will help.

6. Write whatever you want to write early enough so that you can put it away for a period of time and then go over it when you are fresh and have time to evaluate how well you have conveyed your ideas. Make all essential changes, checking particularly to see whether any words or sentences can be eliminated.

SUBJECT

The subject of a sentence is the word or group of words that stands in a precise relationship to the verb. The subject is the element that (1) performs the action expressed by an active verb, (2) receives the action of a passive verb, or (3) is connected to a complement by a linking verb. The subject controls the person and number of the verb. Writers who separate subject from verb by too many words risk violating the rules of agreement, but even when they are lucky enough to get the agreement straight, they usually leave their readers wondering who did what to whom in a sentence.

Subjective Complement

Predicate nouns—also called predicate nominatives—and predicate adjectives function as subjective complements of a linking verb.

She seems *happy* in her work. (predicate adjective)

John characteristically feels *maudlin*. (predicate adjective)

Alice was an active *volunteer*. (predicate noun)

They were paid *assassins*. (predicate noun)

Complements complete linking verbs. Omit the complement of a linking verb, and your sentence will say nothing: *She seems. John feels. Alice was. They were.* The reader is left wondering: *seems what? feels what? was what? were what?* The information needed to complete each thought is missing.

When a previous sentence supplies the missing information, a subjective complement may be omitted:

Who was an active volunteer? *Alice was.* (The subjective complement is understood.)

Who were the paid assassins? *They were.* (Same comment.)

SUBJUNCTIVE MOOD

Largely discarded in English, the subjunctive mood persists in a handful of uses. (See MOOD.)

Condition Contrary to Fact

- If I *were* the leader of this group, I would make sure our meetings ran in a more orderly fashion. (I am not the leader of the group, so *if* introduces a condition that is contrary to fact. The subjunctive *were* is correct.)
- When I *was* the leader, our meetings were orderly. (Since I really was the leader, the indicative *was* is correct.)
- *Were* I twenty years younger, I might have a chance of capturing the attention of undergraduates. (I cannot be younger than I am, so the condition is contrary to fact. The subjunctive *were* is correct.)
- When I *was* twenty years younger, I sometimes could capture their attention. (I once was twenty years younger, so the indicative *was* is correct.)

Verbs of Asking, Recommending, etc.

In formal English, the subjunctive is used in *that* clauses after verbs of asking, demanding, suggesting, and the like.

- The judge recommends that the plaintiffs *withdraw* their suit. (Subjunctive *withdraw* in a *that* clause after a verb of recommending.)
- The committee requested that the delegate *confine* her remarks to the issue under discussion. (Subjunctive *confine* in a *that* clause after a verb of asking.)

In place of *that* clauses requiring the subjunctive, infinitives may be used with verbs of asking, demanding, suggesting, and the like.

- The judge urges the plaintiffs *to withdraw* their suit. (The verb

urges has replaced *recommends*. ("The judge recommends the plaintiff to withdraw their suit" is unidiomatic.)
- The committee asked the delegate *to confine* her remarks to the issue under discussion. (The verb *asked* has replaced *requested*. "The committe requested the delegate to withdraw their suit" is unidiomatic.)

A writer who is in doubt about the use of the subjunctive would do best to avoid it. Time is on that writer's side. The day is not far off when formal English will discard the subjunctive.

SUBORDINATING CONJUNCTION

A subordinating conjunction connects a subordinate clause to an independent clause or to another subordinate clause. Many conjunctions, including *after, because, since, as, as if, so, when, where, why,* and *how* are used for this purpose.

- My wife decided to stay home, *because* she had a deadline to meet. (The subordinating conjunction *because* connects the subordinate clause to the independent clause, *My wife decided to stay home.*)
- I do not know exactly *when* I will be able to return *after* I have done all my errands in the village. (Two subordinating conjunctions: *when* connects the independent clause and the first subordinate clause; *after* connects the two subordinate clauses. Notice that the sentence can be simplified—and improved—by deleting the second subordinate clause and adding *after doing all my errands in the village.*)

The relative pronouns *who, which, what,* and *that* are also used to introduce a subordinate clause.

- I asked the woman *who* originated the idea to come to the platform. (Subordinate clause *who originated the idea*, independent clause *I asked the woman to come to the platform.*)

SUBORDINATION

Subordination is the stylistic practice used to give modifying units the degree of emphasis appropriate to their importance. These modifying units range from single words to lengthy subordinate clauses. Correct subordination helps readers focus attention on the important concepts in writing. Lack of subordination or faulty subordination makes for difficulty in seeing relationships between concepts.

Poor A boycott of the local school was conducted by parents. They demanded that educational standards be maintained. (These two sentences are presented as independent thoughts. Is there no connection between the two concepts? In fact, the concepts are closely related.)

Improved The parents boycotted the school, demanding that educational standards be maintained. (The two sentences have become one. What is now one independent clause, *The parents boycotted the school*, has a verbal modifier, *demanding that educational standards be met*. This change subordinates the concept presented in the second sentence of the original, thereby making clear why the parents boycotted the school. The change has two other benefits. The passive verb *was conducted* has become the active verb *boycotted*, and the logical subject *parents* has been moved into the subject position.)

SUBSTANTIVE

A substantive is a noun, pronoun, or phrase that performs a noun function.

- *Biplanes* became obsolete long ago. (subject of verb)
- Three *candidates* remained under *consideration*. (*candidates*, subject of verb; *consideration*, object of preposition)
- *I* found *three*. (*I*, subject of verb; *three*, object of verb)

SUCH

As an intensifier, *such* is appropriate to informal English, but not to formal English.

Empty Intensifier This was *such* a bad play.
Empty Intensifier They found him *such* a bore.

Empty intensifiers diminish intensity rather than increase it. Without *such*, the two examples state the case simply and dramatically.

Intensifier Removed This was a bad play.
Intensifier Removed They found him a bore.

Notice that the changed sentences do not specify *why* the play was bad or *why* the unidentified *they* found him a bore, but neither do the original versions of the sentences. Perhaps writers should not offer value judgments without an accompanying statement of charges and complete evidence. At any rate, adding the empty intensifier *such* did not make the original statements truer or clearer or more emphatic.

Several formal English constructions employ *such*, but they are generally awkward and should be avoided:

- Their attitude was *such* that the other members of the committee felt obliged to issue a dissent.
- The weather was *such* that the air traffic controllers decided to shut down the airport.

Such in both sentences implies a situation that forces action, but it does not specify what the situation is. It would be better to write:

- The majority report erred in several major sections, so the other members of the committee felt obliged to issue a dissent.
- The rain was so heavy that the air traffic controllers decided to shut down the airport.

SUFFIX

A suffix is an element added to the end of a root or word to make a new word: kind, kind*ly*; fulfill, fulfill*ment*. Suffixes and prefixes together are called *affixes*.

SYNTAX

Syntax is the grammatical relationship among units of a sentence. Defined more broadly, syntax is the rules or patterns found in a language. Followed carefully, the rules and patterns of formal English keep meaning clear. Poor syntax leaves readers guessing.

T

TENSE

Tense is the characteristic of verbs that indicates the time in which the verbs operate. There are three simple tenses (present, past, future) and three perfect tenses (present perfect, past perfect, and future perfect). Except for the simple present and the simple past, most tenses in English are formed with the use of auxiliaries, the principal one being *have*.

Present

The present tense is used to express present actions and states, future actions, habitual actions, and actions and states true for all time.

- He *is* too sick to see you. (present state)
- The ship *sails* at noon tomorrow. (future action)
- He *rides* to work every day. (habitual action)
- All roads *lead* to Rome. (actions true for all time)

Past

The past tense expresses actions completed in the past.

- John *walked* twelve miles last Wednesday.
- The wind *blew* the house down.
- That road *led* to Rome.

Future

The future is expressed by the simple form of the verb with *will* or *shall*. The confusion that has existed over the use of these two auxiliaries has been resolved in colloquial English and largely in general English, both of which now use *will* exclusively. In formal English, *shall* is used for the first person singular and plural, and *will* is used for second and third persons singular and plural. In speech the problem is avoided by use of contracted forms: *we'll, I'll, you'll, she'll*, etc.

The future tense can also be indicated by various idiomatic constructions:

- I am *going to* leave on the 9:45.
- New York City is *about to* rebuild some of its bridges.
- Professor Donner *is to give* the course next year.

Present Perfect

The present perfect indicates that an action begun in the past continues in the present.

- John *has worked* at his job for eight years. (John is still working at his job.)
- Oregon *has* long *been* one of our most scenic states. (It still is.)

Past Perfect

The past perfect distinguishes between the times of two past actions by indicating time prior to past time.

- Deirdre *had worked* at perfecting her ballet form for five years before she finally achieved a satisfactory performance. (She became competent after she *had worked* to perfect her form.)
- Bob *had collected* unemployment insurance for almost three months before he found work. (He found a new job after he *had collected* insurance for months.)

Future Perfect

The future perfect expresses time prior to another future time. The present or future tense is used with the future perfect.

- The virus *will have taken* hundreds of lives by time a satisfactory cure is found. (The future time is expressed here by the present *is found*.)
- The virus *will have taken* hundreds of lives before a satisfactory cure will be found. (The future time is expressed here by the future *will be found*.)

Progressive Tenses

Progressive tenses are also available for ongoing action, action that is in progress. Progressive tenses use the present participle with appropriate auxiliaries.

- I *am enunciating* as clearly as I can. (present progressive— notice that *can*, with *enunciate* understood, is present)
- How long *have* you *been dieting*? (present perfect progressive)
- I *was listening* to music when you called. (past progressive— notice that *called* is past)
- The doctor thought her patient *had been dieting* for at least three months. (past perfect progressive—notice that *thought* is past)
- My mother surely *will be calling* within the hour. (future progressive)
- I *will have been dieting* for most of my life if I live at least ten more years. (future perfect progressive—notice that the future here is expressed by the present, *live*)

The problem of tense can be complicated endlessly, as the foregoing discussion demonstrates.

Remember that tense makes distinctions in time. If there is no need to complicate relationships that are clearly defined, do not complicate them. When you next read anything by Ernest Hemingway, take note of the tenses he uses. You will see how simple a matter tense can be in the hands of an accomplished stylist.

THAN

Than functions both as a conjunction and a preposition.

Conjunction

As a conjunction, *than* introduces clauses of comparison.

- The need for inspection was greater *than* either man had realized.
- The pony was taller *than* Jody. (In this sentence the clause of comparison is implied: *The pony was taller than Jody was.*)

This kind of construction is called *elliptical*. The grammatical significance of an elliptical construction is understood when a pronoun follows *than*. The pronoun in the elliptical clause takes its case from the function performed by the pronoun.

- The pony was taller *than he*. (In this sentence the implied clause of comparison has *he* as its subject: The pony was taller *than he was*.)
- He sees you more often *than me*. (The implied clause of comparison has *me* as its object: He sees you more often *than he sees me*.)

Preposition

As a preposition, *than* requires use of the objective case for its object.

- He knows no one *than whom* he is fonder.
- Sue is a golfer *than whom* I can imagine no one more even-tempered.

Sentences such as these show adherence to grammatical correctness at its worst. Sentences as awkward—albeit correct—as these must be avoided.

In colloquial English, *than* usually takes the objective case, implying that *than* is functioning as a preposition.

Unacceptable in Formal Writing Wilt is taller *than him*. (*Him* must be replaced by *he*.)

Henry is fatter *than her*. (*Her* must be replaced by *she*.)

THAT

That is used as a conjunction, relative pronoun, demonstrative adjective, and adverb.

Conjunction

That is used most frequently as a conjunction introducing an object clause after verbs of seeming, believing, hoping, wishing, and the like.

- All of us hoped *that she could go.*
- John wished *that the operation would be delayed.*

In formal English *that* is usually retained in such clauses, but in general English *that* frequently is omitted.

- All of us hoped *she would go.*
- John wished *the operation would be delayed.*

When more than one *that* clause is used, *that* is usually repeated before each clause to emphasize parallel structure and improve clarity.

- All of us hoped *that* he could go and *that* he could stay for at least one month.
- John hoped *that* the operation would be delayed, *that* another treatment could be found, and *that* he would lose no more time from work.

In general English *that* would not be used in either sentence.

- All of us hoped he could go and could stay for at least one month.
- John hoped the operation would be delayed, another treatment could be found, and he would lose no more time from work.

Relative Pronoun

As a relative pronoun, *that* refers to persons or things, *who* to persons, and *which* to things.

- The book *that* pleases me most year after year is *Portrait of the Artist as a Young Man.*
- A man *who* (or *that*) works hard usually succeeds.
- Jane Austen's first novel, *which* continues to attracted favorable attention, does not appeal to me.

That is used in restrictive modifying clauses, and *which* is used in nonrestrictive modifying clauses. This distinction is losing ground, but it should be retained in formal writing.

- The summer home *that* interested him had been sold. (Without the modifying clause, *that interested him,* the reader would not have adequate identification of *summer house*, so the clause is restrictive.)

- Jill's summer home, *which* she bought three years ago, needs extensive repairs. (The home is sufficiently identified by *Jill's summer home*. For this reason, *which* is used in the modifying clause.)

Demonstrative Adjective

As a demonstrative adjective, *that* indicates or emphasizes choice.

- *that* boy, *that* book, *that* house
- Did you think I meant *that* house?

Adverb

That functions as an adverb in structures such as:

- Will you be there *that* long. (The adverb *that* modifies the adverb *long*.)
- As long as you were willing to work *that* hard, you might at least have taken the time to plan your work. (The adverb *that* modifies the adverb *hard*.)
- Are you really *that* cruel? (The adverb *that* modifies the adjective *cruel*.)

THEN

Then functions both as an adverb of time and as a conjunctive adverb.

- We *then* went on to debate the issue for four more days. (adverb of time)
- Dick worked out for two hours; *then*, tired by his efforts, he lay down in the shadow of the stadium. (conjunctive adverb)

Then must not be confused with *than*.

THERE IS, THERE ARE

In the common constructions *there is* and *there are*, the word *there* is sometimes called an *anticipatory subject*. When an anticipatory subject is used in constructing a sentence, the element that performs the true subject function appears after the verb. In this type of construction, the verb takes its number from the functional subject, not from *there*. The word *there*, which is neither plural nor singular, is not the subject of the verb.

- There *is* a tavern in the town. (*Tavern*, the subject of the verb, is singular, so the verb must be singular.)

- There *were* many taverns in East Rutherford, New Jersey. (*Taverns* is plural, so the verb must be plural.)

Compound Subjects

A compound subject must not be confused with a plural subject. When a verb has a compound subject and the first element of the compound subject is singular, the verb is singular.

- There *is* too much cream and sugar in that coffee for my taste. (The words *cream* and *sugar*, both singular, form a compound subject. Since *cream*, the first element of the compound subject, is singular, a singular verb is used after *there*.)
- *Cream* and *sugar* are used in vast quantities in countries where coffee is drunk. (Now *cream* and *sugar*, two singulars, together form a plural subject, not a compound subject. As a plural subject, *cream* and *sugar* must have a plural verb.)

When the first element of the compound subject is plural, the verb is plural.

- There *are* forks and a napkin in that drawer. (*Forks*, the first element of the compound subject, is plural. A plural verb is used after *there*.)

Turning *there is*, *there are* constructions about will resolve problems of number:

- Too much cream and sugar *is* in that coffee for my taste.
- Forks and a napkin *are* in that drawer.

There is and *there are*—and their stylistic cousin *it is*—make the reader wait for the functional subject, so overuse of these terms leads to flat writing. How often do you use such constructions? To tighten your writing and thereby make it more emphatic, search out all *there is*, *there are*, and *it is* constructions in the first draft of the next paper you write. You should be able to eliminate many of them and, with this simple procedure, achieve substantial improvement in your style.

THING

The word *thing* contributes little meaning to many sentences in which it appears. When *thing* is expendable, it should be eliminated. When another noun is needed in its place, that noun should contribute substantially to meaning.

Unacceptable You did a *thing* I do not like. (What is a *thing*? We will have to wait for an explanation.)

Improved I disapprove of your telling that lie. (Now we know what *thing* meant in the unacceptable sentence—it was not a thing at all. It was a lie or the act of lying. The improved sentence specifies what is meant and requires no further explanation.)

Improved The lie you told your brother disturbs me. (This sentence also stands on its own. The discussion of lying can move on.)

TITLES

Underscore titles of books, magazines, newspapers, book-length poems, motion pictures, plays, operas, works of art, individual spacecraft and aircraft, and ships. Underscored elements appear as italics in printed matter.

Use quotation marks for titles of magazine and newspaper articles, essays, stories, and short poems.

Do not underscore or use quotation marks for titles of book chapters or for a preface or introduction.

Capitalization

The rules for capitalizing words in a title are arbitrary enough to please anybody. **1.** Capitalize all words except articles and prepositions of less than five letters. **2.** Always capitalize the first and last words of a title.

* *Major Barbara*
* *The Taming of the Shrew*
* *A Funny Thing Happened on the Way to the Forum*

Theme Titles

Every school and college paper should have a title, and the best time to write a title is after the paper has been completed. The quality of a title is judged by its appropriateness—does it give readers a good idea of what they will find in the paper? When you read a paper through carefully before writing the title, you will have a good understanding of what the paper will say to an objective reader. Cleverness and catchiness have no place in title writing if they obscure meaning in any way.

TO, TOO, TWO

Is carelessness to blame for the fact that *to*, *too*, and *two* are so often misspelled, even in college themes?

TRANSITIVE AND INTRANSITIVE VERBS

A verb is classified as transitive when it can take an object, as intransitive when it cannot. Many verbs, like *improve,* can be both transitive and intransitive:

> *Transitive* Editing *improved* his novel somewhat. (The object of *improved* is *novel.*)
>
> *Intransitive* He improved gradually after the second week of therapy.

TRANSPOSE

Transpose [⁓] is a frequently used correction mark. It indicates that elements in a sentence or paragraph—even entire sentences or paragraphs—should be moved to improve clarity or emphasis.

TRITE

When preparing the first draft of a paper, writers seldom concern themselves with the quality of their prose. They try instead to get their thoughts down completely and in logical order. Excessive attention to choosing fresh, precise words during this early stage of writing may harm the flow of thought.

Later in the process, particularly during the editing of the first draft, quality of expression becomes a major consideration, second in importance only to quality of reasoning. One goal at this stage should be that of eliminating trite locutions, especially trite metaphors. Triteness has no place in a good paper.

The advice is clear: Replace or cut any expressions you are accustomed to hearing or seeing: *on the spur of the moment, tried and true, by hook or by crook, the whole ball of wax, all nine yards, stiff as a board, strong as an ox, take a back seat,* and thousands more.

U

UNINTERESTED, DISINTERESTED

See DISINTERESTED, UNINTERESTED.

UPPER CASE

Upper-case letters are capital letters; lower-case letters are small letters.

USAGE

When teachers use the word *usage* in criticizing a paper, they are indicating that the marked passage departs from standard English usage. This book is intended to help you correct some errors of usage, but you may also find additional help in your dictionary. (See also MIXED USAGE.)

V

VERB

A verb is a word or group of words that expresses action, state, or a relation between two elements of a sentence—between subject and object or between subject and complement—if an object or complement is present.

VERBAL

Verbals are forms derived from verbs. There are four types of verbals: *present participle, past participle, infinitive,* and *gerund.* The present and past participles are used as adjectives. The infinitive is used as a noun or adjective. The gerund is used as a noun. Verbals take objects and may be modified adverbially.

Present Participle

The *winning* team played exceptionally well in the final game. (*Winning* modifies *team.*)

Our troops conducted themselves honorably in the *losing* battle. (*Losing* modifies *battle.*)

Past Participle

The *unharmed* birds flew out of sight. (*Unharmed* modifies *birds.*)

Ecologists now are experiencing some success as they pursue their *dedicated* work. (*Dedicated* modifies *work.*)

Infinitive

To play seemed more important than eating. (*To play* functions as a noun, subject of the verb *seemed.*)

When Joe and his wife realized that their hosts were tired, they decided *to leave.* (*To leave* functions as object of the verb *decided.*)

He gave me some wild honey *to taste.* (*To taste* functions as an adjective, modifier of the noun *honey.*)

A dream *to dream* sustains most convicts. (*To dream* functions as an adjective, modifier of the noun *dream.*)

Gerund

Many of us prefer *swimming* in an ocean. (*Swimming* functions as object of the verb *prefer* and is modified by *in an ocean.*)

Sliding on the ice may not be a conventional sport, but children enjoy it. (*Sliding* functions as subject of the verb *may be* and is modified by *on the ice*.)

Hazel and Harry are good at *swimming*. (*Swimming* functions as the object of the preposition *at*.)

Although verbals have the appearance of verbs, they do not function as verbs.

Verb-Adverb Combinations

Often an adverb completes the meaning of a verb or is used in combination with a verb to form a new verb. Treat the combination as a verb when the combination has a meaning that is altogether different from the literal meanings of the two words in the combination.

- *Look up* Frank Wodehouse when you get to San Francisco. (The combination *look up* has the meaning "search for," which is quite different from the individual meanings of verb *look* and *up*.)
- When Vera *looks back* at her first marriage, she wonders how she could have made such a mistake. (Another example of a combination having a meaning—returns in thought—that is quite different from the individual meanings of *looks* and *back*.)

VERY

Very is an intensifier so overworked that it has little value.

- They found themselves *very tired* by the end of the day. (Does *very* add anything to *tired* in this sentence? No one knows precisely how tired a tired person is, nor does anyone know how tired a very tired person is.)

It is clear that *tired* can be modified.

- I woke up *tired* this morning, but I am *more tired* now. (This sentence expresses its writer's subjective judgment, and no one can argue about such a judgment.)
- I feel *tired* whenever I am at work, but I feel *most tired* during my trip home. (Again, a writer's valid subjective judgment.)

If *very* were added to either of these sentences, would we know more? *I woke up very tired this morning…. I feel very tired whenever I am at work….* Not much.

Find a better way to intensify feelings or attributes you discuss: *I was so disappointed that I cried* instead of *I was very disappointed*;

she cooked better than the chefs at The Four Seasons instead of *she is a very good cook.*

Under no circumstances should you use *very* with a superlative: *very best, very least,* etc.

VOICE

Voice is the aspect of a verb that indicates the relationship of a subject to the action described by its verb. *Active voice* indicates that the subject is performing the action of the verb; *passive voice* indicates that the subject is acted upon.

Active The car *rammed* the stone wall.

Passive The stone wall *was rammed* by the car.

Active Students finally *opened* their books.

Passive Students' books at last *were opened.*

The passive is formed by using some form of the verb *be* with the past participle. When the passive is used, the grammatical subject position is occupied by the logical object, and the logical subject is relegated to a prepositional phrase or is omitted entirely.

- The carpenter *drove* the final nail into the coffin. (The subject, *carpenter*, is performing the action of *drove*, an active verb.)
- The final nail *was driven* into the coffin by the carpenter. (In this sentence *nail*, the logical object, is emphasized by placing it in the subject position and using a passive verb, *was driven*.)

We can give further emphasis to *nail* by omitting the logical subject *carpenter* entirely:

- The final *nail was driven* into the coffin.

The passive is the voice of choice when its use provides additional emphasis. The following example shows again how the writer changes the point of view of the reader by changing from active to passive.

- Dempsey *knocked* Firpo out of the ring.
- Firpo *was knocked* out of the ring.

In these examples, the writer is confronted by a stylistic decision. Does the writer intend to tell what *Dempsey* did or what happened to *Firpo*?

One characteristic of dull writing is excessive reliance on passive constructions. In your writing, use the passive only when you wish to emphasize the logical object.

W

WHETHER

See IF.

WHICH

The pronoun *which* is used to introduce nonrestrictive modifying clauses.

- The next session of Congress, *which is expected to enact few innovative laws*, will include many veteran legislators.
- Her posthumous work, *which is a novel*, has received poor reviews.

Which should never be used as a catchall to refer vaguely to anything that precedes it. There is a sensible limit to the amount of verbiage a reader can be expected to recall.

- He decided to explain the situation to the policeman once more even though he thought he had explained it all adequately in the first three attempts, *which* was not in agreement with the facts. (*What* was not in agreement with the facts?)
- I had the opportunity to read his first book, *which* I did not know what it was called. (This clumsy use of *which* surely has *book* as its antecedent, but the sentence would be cast better as *I had the opportunity to read his first book, whose title I do not know*.)

In reading transcripts of press conferences of important political figures, we see much naive reliance on *which* and wonder what the pronoun was supposed to mean. Strangely enough, those who attend such press conferences are usually able to understand the intended meaning. The requirements of clear writing are more rigorous than the requirements of speech.

WHO, WHOM, WHOSE

Who is subjective, *whom* objective, *whose* possessive. We confuse these pronouns in our writing because we use them carelessly in conversation.

Pronoun as Object of a Preposition

Incorrect Who are you thinking of? (*Who*, a subjective form, functions incorrectly as the object of the preposition *of*.)

Correct **Whom** are you thinking of? (*Whom*, an objective form, correctly functions as the object of the preposition *of*.)

Correct Of *whom* are you thinking? (Here the preposition *of* immediately precedes the pronoun *whom*, its object, so the relationship is clear. Nobody would write *Of who are you thinking?* Only a pedant would write *Of whom are you thinking?*)

As shown in these examples, the problem of *who* vs. *whom* develops when the preposition *of* is separated from the pronoun.

Relative Pronoun as Object of a Verb

Another pronoun problem develops when a relative pronoun precedes the verb even though the pronoun is the object of the verb:

Incorrect No matter *who* you trust, you are sure to be cheated if you are not careful. (The pronoun *who* functions as the object of the verb *trust*. *Who* is the subjective form, so *whom* must be used.)

Correct No matter *whom* you trust, you are sure to be cheated if you are not careful.

Pronoun as Subject

When *who* is the subject of a relative clause, the verb takes its number from the antecedent of *who*.

- He is one of the few *teachers who take* their vacations in the fall. (The verb *take* is plural because its subject, *who*, refers to *teachers*. Of the teachers *who* take their vacations in the fall, he is one.)
- Al is one of those *lawyers who are* willing to help their clients even if their clients are not rich. (*Lawyers*, a plural, is the antecedent of *who*, so the verb *are* is plural.

Choosing between *who* and *whom* can be troublesome in clauses that have a relative pronoun as subject or object. As a way out of the difficulty, substitute the personal pronoun to determine which relative pronoun to use, *who* or *whom*.

Correct I shall give the money to the man *whom* I designated. (I designated *him*, not *he*.)

Correct The nominee will be the woman *who* gets the most votes in the primary. (*She* gets the most votes.)

Correct The student *who* she says was with her that evening could not be located. (The pronoun *who* is the subject of *was*, not the object of *says*. *She says* is a parenthetic expression that does not affect the pronoun *who*.)

Correct The man *whom* he found asleep in the cabin had no right to be there. (He found *him* asleep in the cabin.)

Whose as Pronoun and as Possessive Adjective

Correct Whose computer survived the electrical storm intact? (*Whose* modifies *computer*, so *whose* is classified as a possessive adjective.)

Correct Whose is the one that survived? (*Whose* functions as subject of the verb *is*, so *whose* is a pronoun.)

WORDINESS

Many writers of earlier times appear to have believed that long sentences lend elegance to style, but modern writers would rather be succinct. Redundant expressions, excessive use of the passive, and deadwood make for wordiness. Examine the following sentences:

Wordy Minorities have been working toward the goal of achieving full civil rights. (Is *toward the goal of* necessary?)

Improved Minorities have been working to achieve full civil rights. (*Toward the goal of achieving* has been reduced to a single word, *achieve*.)

Wordy Putting aside the fact that their children always are dressed and fed adequately, we may yet say the Browns neglect their children in many ways. (*The Browns neglect their children*, the heart of the matter, is buried within language that contributes little to the idea being discussed.)

Improved The Browns neglect their children in many ways, even though they feed and clothe them adequately. (*Putting aside the fact that* and *we may yet say* have been eliminated.)

Such editing contributes to clarity by eliminating unnecessary words and subordinating unimportant ideas. Further, the passive verb *are fed and dressed* in the second example has been replaced by the active *feed and clothe*, and this contributes to the strength of the revision. *The fact that* is always a good candidate for the red pencil, along with *it seems that*, *it should be noted that*, *it was here that*, and their stylistic cousins—all deadwood.

How many words can you eliminate from your writing without hurting the essential meaning? Once you begin to test every sentence you write with this question in mind, you will be on your way to improving your writing.

Y

YOUR, YOU'RE

Your is a possessive adjective.

You're is a contraction of *you are*.

- *Your* car is being repaired. (The car *you own* is being repaired.)
- *Your* notebook was left behind. (The *notebook that belongs to you* was left behind.)
- *You're* going to find that college is much different from high school. (*You are* going to find that college is much different from high school.)
- *You're* sure to find yourself a happier person. (*You are* sure to find yourself a happier person.)